artists for humanity
creative jobs for creative youth

All royalties from the sale of this book go to the organization
Artists for Humanity, afhboston.org.

Artists for Humanity's mission is to bridge economic, racial, and social divisions by providing under-resourced youth with the keys to self-sufficiency through paid employment in the arts.

At the heart of Artists for Humanity is the belief that skills equal power and opportunity. AFH has four goals, which provide urban teens with:

- a **safe, meaningful place** where they are respected for their contributions and develop mentoring relationships that are so important to teens.

- an **opportunity** to have a voice through exhibitions, commercial services, and public presentations.

- the **respect and responsibility** of paid employment that promotes self-esteem and financial accountability. At AFH, young people learn entrepreneurship and get paid for their own creative productions.

- **educational experiences** and support that encourage academic achievement.

Luke Reynolds, EDITOR

Imagine It Better

VISIONS OF WHAT SCHOOL MIGHT BE

HEINEMANN
Portsmouth, NH

Heinemann
361 Hanover Street
Portsmouth, NH 03801–3912
www.heinemann.com

Offices and agents throughout the world

© 2014 by Heinemann

The editor and publisher wish to thank those who have generously given permission to reprint borrowed material:

Excerpts from *A Sand County Almanac* by Leopold. Copyright © 1949, 1977 by Oxford University Press, Inc. Reprinted with permission from Oxford University Press, USA.

Excerpt from blog post "LitWorld Stands UP for Girls" by Pam Allyn, Executive Director, LitWorld. Posted September 23, 2013: http://campaignforeducationusa.org/blog/detail/litworld-stands-up-for-girls. Reprinted with permission from Global Campaign for Education.

Figure 1: Excerpt from the reVOLT Expedition Planner by Peter Hill. Reprinted with permission from the author.

Marc Prensky's essay "The UPLIFT Curriculum: Imagine a New Curriculum That Works for All" copyright © 2014 by Marc Prensky. Reprinted with permission from the author.

"Learning to Teach in the Twenty-First Century" by Linda Darling-Hammond was originally published September 1, 2001, for the George Lucas Foundation. An adapted version appears as "Elena's Story: Envisioning the Making of a Teacher" from http://www.edutopia.org/elenas-story-envisioning-making-teacher. Reprinted with permission from Edutopia of the George Lucas Foundation.

Library of Congress Cataloging-in-Publication Data
Reynolds, Luke.
    Imagine it better : visions of what school might be / Luke Reynolds, Editor.
        pages cm
    Includes bibliographical references.
    ISBN 978-0-325-05373-8
    1. Education—Aims and objectives—United States. 2. Public schools—United States.
3. Educational change—United States. I. Reynolds, Luke. II. Title.

    LA217.2.R4955 2014
    370.973—dc23   2014011674

Editor: Margaret LaRaia
Production: Hilary Goff
Cover and interior designs: Suzanne Heiser
Typesetter: Eric Rosenbloom, Kirby Mountain Composition
Manufacturing: Steve Bernier

Printed in the United States of America on acid-free paper
18 17 16 15 14   PAH   1 2 3 4 5

CONTENTS

FOREWORD

Peter Johnston, The University at Albany—SUNY

Rather than showing test scores to parents, I sometimes think we might do better showing them photographs of their children's faces as they participate in their daily learning activities. The face reveals a great deal about what is going on in the mind, and in that there are real differences among schools and classrooms. Perhaps if parents could look at an array of children's faces from a range of classrooms and decide which face they would like to see on their child, we might inspire a kind of imaginative possibility for schools.

In a recent research project with eighth-grade English language arts teachers, we found that when students are fully engaged, they and their classroom communities are transformed (Ivey and Johnston 2013). And I do not say that lightly. The teachers focused their attention centrally on student engagement. Instead of assigning books to read culminating in book reports, they invited the students to choose from a wide range of personally relevant young adult novels, no strings attached, with only one to three copies of any given title. This relatively small shift toward autonomy and relevance transformed the students' sense of agency, their self-regulation, empathy, identities, and their relational, moral, and intellectual lives. The explosion of conversations around uncertainties created by what the students were reading produced greater trust and more appreciation of differences. Students became less likely to judge and stereotype and more prepared to speak out when they encountered mistreatment of others. And students reported being happier. Yes, happier.

These transformations rendered trivial the increased test scores and diminished differences among subgroup scores. Why? Because children are not merely showing up at school to learn academics, putting their lives on hold until they reach the "college and career" phase. They are living their lives in school and developing as human beings within the social and intellectual life of the school. The fact that students in American schools are largely disengaged (Rampey, Dion, and Donahue 2009) is not merely an intellectual problem, it is an individual mental health problem that metastasizes into a broad array of societal problems.

Many of the essays collected in this book raise questions about what we might count as "the basics," both in educating children and in educating teachers. They raise questions, too, about the legitimate goals of schooling. Even if "college- and career-ready" was an adequate goal of schooling, it would require recognizing that we are teaching people rather than "subjects" — scientists rather than science, mathematicians rather than mathematics. And scientists and mathematicians require a good measure of relational and emotional health, collaborative competence, creativity, moral grounding, and self-direction. As with democracy, preparation for it requires living it.

In my view (Johnston 2012), education is about apprenticing children into humanity and preparing them to advance the human condition, an individual and collective project from which we are, embarrassingly, easily distracted. Conversations about improving education in the United States are impoverished not only because we lose sight of this goal but also because we lack the imagination of what is possible in our schools and classrooms. That is what makes this book important. It offers imaginative possibilities and tools to inspire transformation.

References

Ivey, Gay, and Peter H. Johnston. 2013. "Engagement with young adult literature: Outcomes and processes." *Reading Research Quarterly* 48 (3): 255–275.

Johnston, Peter H. 2012. *Opening Minds: Using Language to Change Lives.* Portland, ME: Stenhouse.

Rampey, B. D., G. S. Dion, and P. L. Donahue. 2009. *NAEP 2008 Trends in Academic Progress* (NCES, 2009–479). Washington, DC: National Center for Education Statistics, Institute of Education Sciences, U.S. Department of Education.

 **Peter Johnston**'s *recent research has focused on the consequences of teachers' classroom talk for the ways children learn and experience themselves and each other, and how engaged reading influences children's social, emotional, moral, and academic development. A member of the International Reading Association's Literacy Research Panel and the Reading Hall of Fame, his book* Choice Words *was recently awarded the P. David Pearson Scholarly Influence Award by the Literacy Research Association for having "demonstrably and positively influenced literacy teaching in classrooms and districts nationally." His most recent book is* Opening Minds.

INTRODUCTION

Luke Reynolds

It's day eleven of the government shutdown. I drive through a national park to go to work each morning, so I don't have to check the news to see whether the government is up and running yet. I just look out my car window and see the orange cones still blocking the entrances to the parking lots. The shutdown is akin to a potent virus for which we've yet to find a vaccine. We stop imagining what *could* happen and start judging one another for what *hasn't* happened. We're quick to point our collective finger at everyone else rather than ask what we might be able to do together.

In education, we see some of the same paralysis that comes from intense judgment and evaluation. As soon as we think one person, one school, one professor, one business leader, one billionaire, one researcher, or one organization has "the answer," we all too quickly begin criticizing and critiquing everyone else. We see scarcity, failure, and strife instead of possibilities for transformation.

Shutting down is the exact opposite of our goal as educators. We walk into our classrooms each morning hoping that *openings* will occur. We hope that our students' minds will open to new possibilities, views, ideas, opportunities, skills, and challenges. We hope that our own hearts will be more open to caring, investing, believing — again — that what seemed impossible yesterday will be obtainable today. We hope that our schools will flourish as places of joy and creativity and challenge and — yes — imagination.

Lewis Hyde, in his poignant and remarkable book *The Gift* (2007), provides a scathing critique of a society that builds itself on principles of shutting down, of scarcity and insufficiency. He writes, "The market-industrial system institutes scarcity, in a manner completely unparalleled and to a degree nowhere else approximated. Where production and distribution are arranged through the behavior of prices, and all livelihoods depend on getting and spending, insufficiency of material means becomes the specific, calculable starting point of all economic activity" (28).

We need to think seriously about the purpose of our schools in this context. Is public education also built on the ideals of a market-industrial system, complete with economic justifications? Or are its intentions deeper, more complex, more fulfilling to both the self and to society? By narrowing conversations of educational purpose to pathways of progress via test scores and standardization alone, we move toward production and distribution. We quantify inputs and outputs and try to increase the rates of these inputs and outputs as if human connection and growth can be reduced to an equation.

The writers of the essays in this book reject simple equations and product-distribution mindsets. Instead, they are re-envisioning possibilities. They are not interested in profits — in "getting and spending" — but rather are empowered by the goal of improving the lives of students, teachers, and society at large. What if instead of beginning with a scarcity mindset that causes students, teachers, parents, administrators, and others invested in education to shut down, we start with an *imaginative* mindset? What if we imagine education as we want it to be, remembering that education is, at its core, about people and relationships, not about "getting and spending"?

Diane Ravitch (2010) powerfully warns that "the schools will surely be failures if students graduate knowing how to choose the right option from four bubbles on a multiple-choice test, but unprepared to lead fulfilling lives, to be responsible citizens, and to make good choices for themselves, their families, and our society" (224). If we always begin with blame over test scores and chastisement about what our tax dollars are "getting" us as a society, we will be lost in a perpetual cycle of scarcity. We may enable students to score better on bubble tests, but the goal of guiding them to lead fulfilling lives and creating a responsible, just society will recede farther in our rear-view mirror. We need to return to the elemental questions, imagine how school could be — what we want school to create and what we believe it should do — and propose the most inspired and inspiring ways to achieve these possibilities.

This goal recognizes the structural inequalities inherent in a system of education that is based on "getting and spending," one that views success as correct answers rather than authentic growth, social equality, and transformation. Asking one another to re-envision what we expect of schools is not easy, and there is a layer of privilege in even having the time and resources to pose these kinds of questions. Yet there is a great responsibility to do so, lest our privilege march onward toward profit and even oppression. If we take seriously the call to educate students, we need to imagine how knowledge can be viewed differently, how we can create it differently, how we hear it, explain it, share it, and — especially — how we *count* it.

Poet Mary Oliver (1998) asks a hard question that deserves an honest response from educators, administrators, and policymakers: "Listen, are you breathing just a little, and calling it a life?" We can blame and criticize one another, point fingers, and advocate for a thousand mini-shutdowns throughout our educational system. Or we can start imagining other possibilities and share those possibilities in ways that empower and inspire. We can work toward re-envisioning what counts as knowledge and forge new paths rather than walk those dictated by market-industrialism.

Just as one rain shower will not grow a field of flowers, one person or group will not devise a plan that transforms our educational system perfectly. But if we can learn to offer ideas grounded in imagination, grown with hope, and empowered by action and belief, we will be well on our way toward creating something new. As Hyde tells us, "The passage into mystery always refreshes. If, when we work, we can look once a day upon the face of mystery, then our labor satisfies" (25). It is time for us to be refreshed by diving into *what could be*, and in order to do so we must tell Scarcity and Status Quo that their time at the table of education is through. We need to invite Imagination to sit with us, knowing full well that while things might get messy, these ideas will lend strength to our hands and freshness to our ideas: our labor will deeply satisfy.

Out of this hope for and commitment to transformative action comes the book you hold in your hands. From Sonia Nieto's poignant and insightful assignment asking her students to explore what makes an ideal school to Marilyn Cochran-Smith and Rebecca Stern's exploration of inquiry as a remarkable and eye-popping way to gaze on the world, our students, and ourselves to Samantha Bennett's humorous and profound exploration of collaboration and coaching throughout a school district, each essay is a story about *what could be* and each story has the heartbeat of imagination. The authors here are seeking to go beyond describing the past or repeating the present; they are willing to look deeply into Hyde's mystery to describe something we can't quite yet see and sometimes we can't believe could ever exist.

What is required of us in this moment is to open up, not shut down. We need to look honestly and reflectively at ourselves, our public education system, and our means. Instead of viewing each with a scarcity mindset bent on highlighting failures and worshipping bubble tests, we need to focus on the overwhelming surplus that is — right now — part of public education. In what specific ways do authentic human connections lead students and teachers to incredible growth? How do empowering, justice-oriented teaching methods transform classrooms? In what ways can — and do — classrooms create new cultures and possibilities rather than recapitulate old ones? And how do we close our ears to the numbing refrain of criticism and fear so we can see with fresh vision the incredible human capacity for transformation before us?

The essays in this book do just that.

References

Hyde, Lewis. 2007. *The Gift*. New York: Random House.

Oliver, Mary. 1998. *West Wind: Prose and Prose Poems*. New York: Mariner Books.

Ravitch, Diane. 2010. *The Death and Life of the Great American School System*. New York: Basic Books.

 **Luke Reynolds** *currently teaches seventh-grade English in the public school system in Harvard, Massachusetts. He is a husband, father, activist, writer, teacher, and researcher who is passionate about creative, relational, and imaginative education. Luke is the author of* A Call to Creativity *and the co-editor of* Burned In: Fueling the Fire to Teach; Dedicated to the People of Darfur: Writings on Fear, Risk, and Hope; *and* Break These Rules.

PART 1

Imagine a School Environment That Reflects the World We Want to Live In

The Future of Learning

Tony Wagner

Beginning about one hundred years ago, countries in Europe and North America developed assembly line "factory schools" for their emerging industrial economies. The goal was to "batch process" large numbers of people so that they might gain basic skills. Since then, the world has changed profoundly while schools have remained largely the same. Reimagining schools for work, learning, and citizenship in the twenty-first century must be our highest priority. As we think about education in the future, two new realities stand out:

1. The notion of work is being transformed at an extraordinary pace. Even highly skilled routine jobs are now being automated or sent offshore, and this trend will continue to accelerate dramatically.

2. Knowledge has become a free commodity. It's growing exponentially and is available on every Internet device. As a result, you no longer need to go to school to acquire content knowledge, and there is no competitive advantage in having acquired more knowledge than the person next to you. He or she will find what is needed to solve a problem, get a job done, or create new knowledge.

The net result of these two trends is that the world no longer cares *how much* you know. What the world cares about is what you can *do* with what you know. The capacity to innovate, to solve problems creatively, and to use critical-thinking, communication, and collaboration skills matter far more than academic knowledge. As one executive told me, "We can teach new hires the content, and we will have to because it continues to change, but we can't teach them how to think — to ask the right questions — and to take initiative."

Every young person will, of course, still need to learn content knowledge. However, they will need to learn skills and motivation even more. Of these three education areas, motivation is the most critical — and it is the one we do most damage to with our current forms of schooling. Young people who are intrinsically motivated — curious, persistent, and willing to take risks — will learn new knowledge and skills consistently. More importantly, they will be able to find new opportunities or create their own — a disposition that will become increasingly important as traditional careers disappear. While conducting research for my latest book, *Creating Innovators: The Making of Young People Who Will Change the World*, I've come to understand the importance of play, passion, and purpose in reinforcing intrinsic motivation in both learning and work.

In most schools today, we spend far too much time teaching and testing things most students have no interest in and will never need — like Algebra II and beyond — or facts that they can find easily on the Internet and will likely forget as soon as the test is over. As a result, the longer kids are in school, the less motivated they become. In a 2013 US survey conducted by Gallup, student engagement went from 80 percent in fifth grade to only 40 percent in high school. There is no reason to think that these results would vary significantly in EU countries, as the nature of schooling there is quite similar to ours.

Students will increasingly turn to online sources for the content knowledge they need. As a result, the value added by teachers will be transformed. Teachers will need to become coaches — coaching students to performance excellence. The best principals will continue to be instructional leaders, individuals who know what good teaching looks like and who can coach for sustained improvement of teaching.

However, they will also need to learn how to create the culture of collaboration, trust, and respect that is required for innovation.

Assessment and accountability must also be transformed to align with these education goals. Students will need to develop digital portfolios that follow them through school, where they show evidence of mastery of skills such as critical thinking and communication, reflection on their work, and setting new learning goals. College professors and employers will audit random graduate's portfolios for quality and to help them establish performance standards, which can then be mapped backward for earlier grades. Selective use of high-quality skills tests, like the College and Work Readiness Assessment, will be important. (More information on the CWRA can be found at http://cae.org/performance-assessment/category/cwra-overview.) Finally, teacher effectiveness ought to be judged on evidence of improvement in students' oral and written work throughout the year instead of on scores obtained on a two-hour bubble test at the end of the school year.

Performance standards — not content standards — must become the new normal throughout the education system. We will also come to see that, in the words of Albert Einstein, "what counts can't always be counted." Collective human judgment, informed by evidence, is a far more reliable way to assess the qualities that matter most in students' work — just as it is in the business world. Google famously used to hire students only from brand-name colleges with the highest GPAs and test scores. However, according to recent interviews with Laszlo Bock, Senior Vice President of People Operations at Google, these data are "worthless" as predictors of employee effectiveness at Google. The company now looks for evidence of a sense of mission and personal autonomy and is increasingly hiring people who do not have a college degree (Lazlo 2013, Lohr 2013).

To bring this re-envisioned education system to life, we must begin investing in educational R&D (research and development). Imagine creating lab schools where students earn a high school diploma by completing a series of hands-on, skill-based "merit badges" in things like entrepreneurship. What if we reinvented teacher training so that all new teachers were required to have extended "residencies" with master teachers in lab schools and work with these teachers to develop new approaches to teaching and assessment. We could certify new teachers on the basis of good teaching as evidenced in their digital portfolios.

As we look to the future, there are a growing number of exciting models from which we can learn a great deal. Finland is a country where the majority of students leave high school "innovation-ready" (Pasi 2012). They master concepts and creativity more than facts and have a choice of many electives — all with a shorter school day, very little homework, and almost no testing. In tenth grade, students choose between an academic or a career/technical/vocational track, which has been developed in close collaboration with businesses. Both lead to postsecondary educational choices. The result is that Finland's economy is now more highly rated on indices of innovation and entrepreneurship than ours. And it spends less per student than we do.

In the United States, five hundred K–12 schools affiliated with the Hewlett Foundation's Deeper Learning initiative, along with a consortium of more than 130 school districts — called EdLeader21 — are developing new approaches to teaching, learning, and assessment. There are also a growing number of "reinvented" colleges, like the Franklin W. Olin College of Engineering, the MIT Media Lab, and the d.school at Stanford, where students engage in interdisciplinary, project-based courses that are frequently focused on understanding and trying to find solutions to real-world problems. The students also do most of their work in teams and, as a result, master skills needed to innovate.

Teachers don't have to wait for permission to implement many of these changes in their classrooms. Teachers can start now by incorporating more rich and challenging academic content in their lessons while teaching the skills that matter most. They can also begin using digital portfolios to document their students' developing skills — beginning with the Four C's: Critical Thinking, Communication, Collaboration, and Creative Problem-solving. Edleader21 teams have developed rubrics that teachers can use to assess these critical competencies, which will soon be available on their website: www.edleader21.com. Finally, teachers can give students class time to pursue their own learning interests, to ask their own questions, to design their own investigations, or just explore something that interests them — and the students can document their learning in their digital portfolios. Google and other companies have found that many of their most important innovations have come from giving their employees 15 to 20 percent of their time to work on any project of their choice. Perhaps the most important thing teachers can do is to bring more play, passion, and purpose into every lesson plan.

What can business leaders do to generate momentum to transform the education system? Lew Gerstner, the CEO of IBM, and David Kearns, the CEO of Xerox, led several national summits on education in the United States in the 1990s, which resulted in pressure on lawmakers to create what I call Accountability 1.0 (Wagner 2012). We urgently need new national and state education summits in the United States, led by the next generation of business, community, and education leaders, who can help define what it means to be an educated adult in the twenty-first century. These leaders can work with educators to advocate for new accountability systems that will be aligned with the outcomes that matter most.

References

Bryant, Adam. 2013. "In Head-Hunting, Big Data May Not Be Such a Big Deal." *New York Times*, June 19, 2013. www.nytimes.com/2013/06/20/business/in-head-hunting -big-data-may-not-be-such-a-big-deal.html. Accessed October 3, 2013.

Lohr, Steve. "Big Data, Trying to Build Better Workers." *New York Times*, April 20, 2013. www.nytimes.com/2013/04/21/technology/big-data-trying-to-build-better-workers.html. Accessed October 3, 2013.

Sahlberg, Pasi. 2012. *Finnish Lessons: What can the world learn from educational change in Finland?* New York: Teachers' College Press.

Wagner, Tony. 2012. *Creating Innovators: The Making of Young People Who Will Change the World.* New York: Scribner.

A former high school teacher, **Tony Wagner** *is the author of five books on education, most recently* Creating Innovators *and* The Global Achievement Gap. *Both continue to be best sellers. He currently serves as Expert in Residence at Harvard's new Innovation Lab. Tony can be reached via Twitter: @DrTonyWagner or via his website: www.tonywagner.com.*

Imagine the End of Ranking

Andy Hargreaves

In the fall of 2013, the Organization for Economic Cooperation and Development (OECD) released its Program for International Student Assessment (PISA) scores of educational achievement, country by country, into the midst of another global media frenzy. The Americans and Brits bemoaned another paltry performance against international opposition. The Finns started to fall. Their neighboring Swedes continued to languish below them. Canadian provinces inexplicably exchanged places in the rankings. Countries at the bottom started to move up, challenging commentators to find explanations for this shift other than the likelihood that the initially poorest performers were experiencing regression to the mean. Meanwhile the children and teachers of Asian countries and cities — South Korea, Singapore, Shanghai, Hong Kong — put their Western counterparts to shame.

Pundits proffered all manner of preferred explanations for the ups and downs of the scores. For OECD's Andreas Schleicher, it's a fact that high-performing nations really engage their learners, though he used to say it was because they had high-quality teachers, and before that, that they all had a coherent, centrally directed strategy. Thomas Friedman claims it's because the high performing nations promote teacher ownership of learning and change, though he oddly blames only US unions and not, say, the US government and its teacher evaluation strategies, for preventing this. Many have attributed Asian success to an ethic of hard work, discipline, and extra time devoted to learning — the very factors that people gave to explain Japan's success during its educational and economic booms in the 1990s, but which went out of fashion when the Japanese economy collapsed.

The reactions to previous waves of PISA results have precipitated massive shifts in national educational policy, and the 2013 wave of results will be no different. For example, between 2006 and 2009, Australia fell from sixth to ninth on PISA results in reading. This prompted a national push to be in the top five by 2025. Yet, in the meantime, three additions had been made to the list (Singapore, Hong Kong, and Shanghai), and all of them were in the new top five. So in relation to the original list, Australia hadn't fallen at all, but it was still driving a massive 12-year reform to move up just one place from sixth to fifth.

The Netherlands also wants to be back in the top five. So does Ireland. This tiny PISA pedestal is clearly going to be a very crowded one. Wales declares it wants to be in the PISA top 20 (another way of saying it wants to be above Scotland) within just two years — a goal that also instigated a massive reform drive within the country. Whatever the actual merits of PISA as an indicator — and it's one I have also used a lot over the years — the policy upheaval that takes place because of it in country after country is undesirable and unwarranted. Here are six reasons why.

1. Negative or Troubling Indicators Are Overlooked

The high PISA performers of Singapore, Korea, and Japan have cultures that support intensive after-school tutoring services. So does this mean that American or British students should now be doing extra cramming and test prep long into the night? Korea has such examination fever, as it calls it, that children have practically no spare time, and even that may be dedicated only to an hour or two of video gaming late into the night. The high PISA performers of Finland, Singapore, and Korea have widespread military service for men, which could be one possible contributor to strong national identity. So should the United States and Britain re-introduce compulsory military service? Finland has very high rates of male alcoholism and suicide. Korea has some of the highest youth suicide rates in the world. Young Japanese people have become so stressed by the relentless quest for achievement that defined their parents' generation that they have become increasingly disinterested in sex, marriage, and intimacy. These may be successful societies in terms of educational achievement, but according to some key criteria, they are also profoundly sick ones. Are they the kinds of societies the rest of us truly want to be emulating?

2. Interpretations Are Limited by the OECD's Mandates

The OECD, which produces the PISA results, has a mandate to meet the needs and requirements of the Ministers of the countries who fund them and provide their terms of reference. These terms of reference are not educationally inclusive. For instance, the OECD has no mandate to address issues of curriculum. So, although it could well be the case that mathematical achievement in Singapore is highly attributable to its globally admired curriculum, this is scarcely mentioned by the OECD because curriculum is not part of its mandate. The OECD also has no mandate to discuss or develop special education strategies and reforms. This means that while the special education policies in many high-performing Asian countries are 30 years or more behind the United States, and may influence which students are included in PISA's test samples (to the comparative advantage of these Asian countries), these policies receive no discussion in OECD's presentation or in other people's discussion of the PISA results. The OECD is limited by its mandates in terms of what it foregrounds or ignores, meaning that certain recommended policy strategies become priorities not because of their inherent superiority but because of their compatibility with those mandates.

3. Indicators Are Highlighted Selectively

Policy mandates and ideological preferences too often lead to some factors being privileged over others as explanations for national educational success. Such an example is raised by the Brown Center on Education Policy at the Brookings Institution. It describes how some commentators attribute Poland's recent dramatic achievement gains made on the PISA tests to the country's abolition of tracking students by ability. However, the report says:

Poland's 1999 education reforms were not limited to tracking. Instead, they involved a complete overhaul of the Polish school system, including decentralization of authority and greater autonomy for schools, an increase in teacher salaries, a new system of national assessment, adoption of a core curriculum and national standards, reform of teacher education at the university level, and a new system of teacher promotion. Any one of these policies — or several in combination — may have produced Poland's gains on PISA. Some may have even produced negative effects, dragging down achievement, while others offset the losses with larger gains. The point is this: no single reform can be plucked from several reforms adopted simultaneously and declared to have had the greatest positive impact. Not based on PISA data. The data do not allow it. (Loveless, 2012, pp. 28–29)

4. Other Indicators Are Ignored or Avoided

The PISA rankings are not the only indicator of educational achievement or success. On other indicators, such as the International Mathematics and Science Studies (TIMMS) or the Progress in International Reading Literacy study (PIRLS), the successful countries are not always those that perform well on PISA. Russia, for instance, is a top performer according to PIRLS, but this status has not led to an international charge to copy the Russians' education system. A number of Eastern European countries do quite well on math and science, but there is no worldwide urge to emulate them either. Then there are UNICEF's indicators of children's well-being at age fifteen in terms of health, housing, economic security, mental health, and so on. Asian countries do not appear in these UNICEF data, though many, such as Singapore, do very poorly on other indicators of health and well-being. Indeed, international comparisons of relationships between social inequality and outcomes of health and well-being reveal that the "selfish capitalism" of more market-driven, Anglo-American public systems is associated with greater inequalities and negative health outcomes than the "selfless capitalism" of many continental European systems (Wilkinson and Pickett 2009; James 2008). We need to take the PISA rankings into account *in relation to* many other indicators, so that even if we still value high performance on PISA, we can discern better and worse paths to high PISA performance that either support or undermine other aspects of quality of life such as mental health, absence of obesity, social equity, and opportunity.

5. Other Spurious Indicators Are Invented

One response to the relentless onslaught of PISA results that consistently rank the United Kingdom and United States as poor performers has been to concoct other indicators of international achievement. Such indicators include factors like university performance and prestige, which then suddenly catapult the United States and United Kingdom to the top rather than the lower and middle reaches of the rankings. From the perspective of economic interest, these alternate rankings are used to prop up Anglo-American versions of competitive individualism in capitalism and competitive educational achievement against Asian and Northern European alternatives (McKinsey, Economist).

6. PISA Prep Is Becoming Prevalent

With the affordance of materials provided by the OECD, it is now increasingly possible for individual schools to rank and rate themselves on PISA items, and to prepare their students by taking PISA-like test items in order to boost their own performance. One rationale for this is so schools and countries can develop the skills that PISA values. Another eventual and unavoidable effect, though, is that this will essentially introduce teaching to the test on a global scale. At that point, the very criterion that gave PISA more credibility than internal national tests (it was not an assessment system that countries could manipulate) will be eliminated, and the entire legitimacy of PISA will be undermined. Thus far, the announcement of the PISA results has been a weighty drama of international policy proportions. In future years, it will likely turn into little more than a media circus.

The Alternative?

So what should we do instead? Many of the answers are already implicit in the critique I have just set out. Put PISA in perspective. Consider what is out of the

OECD's mandate, as well as what is in it. Don't jump to conclusions to suit your own political or educational ideology. Acknowledge that there are different paths to PISA excellence, and choose the ones that are superior on the grounds of other educational and child development factors. Don't rely on PISA alone. And don't turn PISA — or any other measure — into a test you can prepare for to game the system, distort your priorities, or fabricate results.

Do strive for values beyond measured attainment. Learn from others, but do not let this learning be limited or defined by national borders. Don't hold our children hostage to a competition being ruthlessly driven by powerful adults. Put engagement in learning and teaching before achievement in results, and make it the path to achieving those results. Value happiness, kindness, compassion, and joy as well as intellectual success. Keep a balanced scorecard of human development. Make these educational rights into global human rights from which there are no national or religious exclusions.

Concentrate on the qualities that unite us and the differences that delight us, not on the rankings that incite us into policy upheaval, attacks on educational professionals, and a narrowing of the educational experiences in school that, for every child, can never be returned to or repeated. The children become the parents of their country and their communities. Begin properly with the child and we will need no competition between countries any more. Imagine.

 **Andy Hargreaves** *is the Thomas More Brennan Chair in the Lynch School of Education at Boston College. The mission of the Chair is to promote social justice and connect theory and practice in education.*

~~Save~~ See the Forest and Think Like a Mountain

Sandy Grande

> A deep chesty bawl echoes from rimrock to rimrock, rolls down the mountain, and fades into the far blackness of the night. It is an outburst of wild defiant sorrow, and of contempt for all the adversities of the world. Every living thing (and perhaps many a dead one as well) pays heed to that call . . . . Only the mountain has lived long enough to listen objectively to the howl of a wolf.
>
> — Aldo Leopold, *A Sand County Almanac*

Introduction

I began this essay with a quote from Aldo Leopold's classic text *A Sand County Almanac* (1949) because his observation that "only the mountain has lived long enough to listen objectively to the howl of a wolf" is an apposite reminder that understanding the strength, beauty, and fragility of ecosystems is an important first step to enacting pedagogies of wholeness and generosity. While good teachers know this intuitively, they are immersed in educational climates where individualism and avarice prevail. The field is dominated by educational reformers who can't see the forest for the trees and, even more perniciously, are actively engaged in educational deforestation — sacrificing the long-term health and well-being of communities for short-term, individualist gains.

Educational deforestation is an agenda fueled by the "remove to replace" logic of settler colonialism[1] (Wolfe 2006), under which schools have experienced clear-cutting of curricula, slashing and burning of budgets, and an exploitation of local human and material resources for private gain. Worse yet, the agenda has been cynically enacted under the guise of democracy and "saving" our children. The problem is that neither children nor forests need "saving" — a messianic act that typically involves top-down agendas. Rather, they need *seeing;* an act of radical love predicated on close examination, openness to experience, empathy, and care. Forests, like classrooms, are life-giving only insofar as the complex network of systems and relations that sustain them are cultivated and appreciated. So my message, my hope for teachers, is that we join forces against the capitalist brutalities of austerity and immiseration, and organize instead a mass movement of restoration — to see the forest and think like a mountain.

Given the current import of Leopold's message, I have reproduced sections of his essay to serve as introductions to the different segments of this chapter. The first segment begins with naming the agents, causes, and effects of deforestation; not to call undue attention to the negative, but rather to underscore how the elision of root causes denies us the depth of experience needed to inform positive agendas of transformation. In the second segment, I offer some beginning thoughts on how to construct a new horizon for teaching, one defined by "thinking like a mountain."

Seeing the Forest: Agents, Causes, and Effects

. . . Only the ineducable tyro can fail to sense the presence or absence of wolves, or the fact that mountains have a secret opinion about them.

My own conviction on this score dates from the day I saw a wolf die . . .

I realized then, and have known ever since, that there was something new to

---

1 While it falls outside the bounds of this essay to discuss the historic continuities of settler colonialism, suffice it to say that what began as a political project contingent upon the elimination of indigenous peoples in order to appropriate indigenous land has persisted through the forces of accumulation by dispossession or what Wolfe (2006) has termed the "logic of elimination."

me in those eyes — something known only to her and to the mountain. I was young then, and full of trigger-itch; I thought that because fewer wolves meant more deer, that no wolves would mean hunters' paradise. But after seeing the green fire die, I sensed that neither the wolf nor the mountain agreed with such a view.

In this section of his essay, Leopold recounts his own experience as a "tyro"[2] hunter, an unwitting agent of deforestation, seduced by opportuneness and the false promise that "more always means more." In the realm of education, there are hunters of a different kind. Policy makers, legislators, politicians, and corporate actors — all "full of trigger-itch" — take aim at teachers, driven by the belief that if fewer unionized teachers means fewer "barriers to change" (read: profit) that no teachers at all is a reformer's paradise. However, like the young hunters in Leopold's essay, school reformers fail to sense either "the presence or absence" of teachers and the complex role they play in the delicate ecosystem of a school.

The removal of teachers is just one strategy in a privatization agenda known in school-reform parlance as "portfolio management." As Hing (2012) reports, "while portfolio management looks different from city to city," it generally employs neoliberal strategies (e.g., deregulation, decentralization, and reduction of the public sphere), manufacturing crisis and then opportunity for private operators to "take over." In the educational marketplace, districts and schools are commodified, treated like stocks — traded, closed, or expanded based on their "performance" (Hing 2012).

Cities such as Newark, Chicago, New Orleans, Seattle, Philadelphia, Hartford, and New York have all endured the brutalities of portfolio management. They are, however, also hotbeds of resistance because, as it turns out, schools are not stocks (Hing 2012). They are community institutions with deep roots that cannot easily be dismantled and closed. Neither can students, teachers, and administrators be painlessly traded from one community to another; they resist because they are human beings, not commodities.

---

2 In this context, "tyro" means *beginner* or *neophyte*.

Since then I have lived to see state after state extirpate its wolves. I have seen every edible bush and seedling browsed, first to anaemic desuetude, and then to death . . .

I now suspect that just as a deer herd lives in mortal fear of its wolves, so does a mountain live in mortal fear of its deer. And perhaps with better cause, for while a buck pulled down by wolves can be replaced in two or three years, a range pulled down by too many deer may fail of replacement in as many decades.

Similarly, in the wake of reform, school districts across the nation have dwindled to "anaemic desuetude." The profound mismanagement and callous treatment of human and material resources has plummeted already precarious communities into even deeper states of social and economic crisis. A school may be able to be replaced momentarily by a storefront charter, but an entire district pulled down by profit-hungry reformers leaves behind human dustbowls that will take generations to remedy.

While the process of removal has been greatly accelerated by reformists, we — the guardians of the public sphere — are not without fault. Whether through the politics of obedience, blind faith, conformity, fatigue, recalcitrance, or self-satisfaction, we have failed to disrupt the settler project and the myth of meritocracy upon which it feeds. That is, we accepted the convenient fiction that test scores and evaluations equate with cognitive ability and competency, and therefore that winners and losers have been created by their own making.

To avoid complicity, we need to remind each other, and ourselves, that there is no inevitability to this project and refuse the capitalist dictum that there is no alternative. Courageous public school warriors, such as Helen Gym, Karen Lewis, Valerie Strauss, Wendy Lecker, Thomas Scarice, Beth Sondel, Pauline Lipman, Curtis Acosta, Antony Cody, Wayne Au, Carol Burris, Joesph Rella, Mercedes Schneider, Valerie Shirley, and Jeremy Garcia, among countless others, demonstrate each and every day alternative visions for schools and communities.

Thinking Like a Mountain: Pedagogies of Wildness

We all strive for safety, prosperity, comfort, long life, and dullness. The deer strives with his supple legs, the cowman with trap and poison, the statesman with pen, the most of us with machines, votes, and dollars, but it all comes to the same thing: peace in our time. A measure of success in this is all well enough, and perhaps is a requisite to objective thinking, but too much safety seems to yield only danger in the long run. Perhaps this is behind Thoreau's dictum: In wildness is the salvation of the world. Perhaps this is the hidden meaning in the howl of the wolf, long known among mountains, but seldom perceived among men.

Schooling and teaching have been eternally bound by too much "safety" — the canned curricula, whitewashed textbooks, results-driven assessments, and rote pedagogies. Which is not to say that teachers have been uninspired or lazy or bad, but rather to reveal institutionalization as yet another mode of structural adjustment, a regulative contraction of resources that in and of itself conflates learning with recall. Warriors for education fight for schools and communities that thrive beyond the traps of "safety, prosperity, comfort, long life, and dullness." They understand — they *see* — that the horizon of social justice is not high grades and test scores for all, nor is it an uncomplicated vision of "the good life." Rather, it is rooted "in wildness."

Within the current structure and climate of education, warrior teaching is a political act that requires taking a stance against institutionalization and actively working toward reinserting meaning, risk-taking, playfulness, imagination, and enchantment back into learning. Specifically, warrior teachers are those who:

- embrace learning as messy, paradigm-shifting, consciousness raising, somatic
- operate beyond and between traditional disciplinary boundaries in order to highlight the connection and relationships among diverse funds of knowledge

- work against the culture of consumerism, the tedium of the necessary and urgent (trigger-itch), and aspire to ontological knowing

- reject "settler logics" of individualism, competition, accumulation, and immediate return and instead embrace pedagogies of connectedness, cooperation, generosity, and thinking long-term

- resist knowledge as "production" and see knowledge as a "relationship" — to place, to history, to self, to other, to community, and to higher senses of being — in other words, to mountains.

If warrior teaching is the political practice, then enchanted learning is the horizon. In enchanted classrooms, the focus is on systems and connections, wherein students may study the math of climate change, the chemistry in and of their lives, the history of their neighborhoods, literature of bliss, and art as a form of resistance and protest. More than anything this kind of teaching takes time and is not easily measured. Thus, particularly in this historical moment, it should be noted that whenever and wherever it happens, warrior teaching is heroic. Joined in force, however, we can support each other and create structures that enable us to see the forest, and ~~think~~ teach like a mountain.

Sandy Grande *is an Associate Professor and Chair of the Education Department at Connecticut College (appointed member). She also serves as a member of the National Environmental Justice Advisory Council's (NEJAC) Indigenous People's Work Group (IPWG). Sandy's research and teaching is profoundly inter- and cross-disciplinary and interfaces critical and Indigenous theories with the concerns of education. Her book,* Red Pedagogy: Native American Social and Political Thought *is currently being published in a tenth-anniversary edition. She has also published several book chapters and articles*

including, "Accumulation of the Primitive: The Limits of Liberalism and the Politics of Occupy Wall Street," The Journal of Settler Colonial Studies; *"Confessions of a Fulltime Indian,"* Journal of Curriculum Studies, The Journal of Curriculum and Pedagogy; *"American Indian Geographies of Identity and Power: At the Crossroads of Indigena and Mestizaje,"* Harvard Educational Review; *and, "Red-ding the Word and the World," in* Paulo Freire's Intellectual Roots: Toward Historicity in Praxis.

Schooling with a Present and Future Purpose

A Letter to the Next Generation

Eve Tuck

with Michelle Belina, Jason Betley, Ryan Brosi, Hayden Carlin, Jesse Cersosimo, Fatima Elmouchtari, Jason Gambino, Brian K. Jones, Alexander Klein, Anna Kowal, John Mazzoni, Jessica Pierorazio, Chase Randell, Khallid Utley, and Roy Verspoor

This essay was composed at the close of a Social Foundations of Education graduate course at the State University of New York at New Paltz. Eve, who taught the course and was expecting a baby at the time, wrote the parts in regular type. The students in the course, who had varied experiences in schools and as educators, wrote the portions in bold type together. The essay addresses the next generation — literally, in Eve's case. It responds to themes in the course's readings and conversations, especially with regard to what the resulting imagined school looks and feels like, perspectives on learning, school leadership and visioning, the work of teachers, and teacher education.

This is the school I imagine for you before you are even born.

School is a place outside our home. You go to school outside our home while I go to work, because I like my work and I like to go to work. I also like your school, and sometimes I go to school with you. You may work alongside me there, or maybe as you are going about your own activities, you will see me through the large glass window you pass by in the hallway, reading in a comfortable chair or working at a computer. You have your own compelling work to do, so sometimes you will just wave and smile, acknowledging that we share this space.

Your school is a place where families can come to spend part of their day, reading, writing, gardening, making art and music, making pottery, learning languages, and dancing. Your school is one of many hubs of life in our community — there are other lively places in our world where we receive care and services. We visit your school — to attend community events, to work together on projects, to learn new things — when we have time.

Perspectives on Learning

Your teachers love and respect you and our family. They know students learn best from people who love and respect them. They do not resent you, and they do not wish you would be quiet. They help you become more of who you are. They teach you to become a lifelong learner and try to inspire an enduring love of learning in all their students. Your teachers help you to see that learning is not accumulation, it is not consumption, and it is not hoarding. Learning is not stingy or jealous. Learning is not domination, assimilation, deculturation. Learning does not try to make you into a colonizer, a settler on stolen land.

Your learning is contextual in the present, but it anticipates the future. It is also reciprocal; the teacher gives you what you need and receives new understanding from that transaction. Some things cannot be known by everyone. For example, there are things that I will teach you that my grandmother and mother taught me — those things are for us, for Unangax̂ people, and not for everyone to know. We take care of the sacred knowledge that is shared with us: it makes us who we are.

School Leadership and Visioning

There are professional leaders at your school who have learned how to be courageous in the face of wayward and demeaning policies. Your school leaders understand that schools are shaped by social policies related to health care, housing, transportation, taxation, and labor. They understand that sometimes schools are asked to do more than they can do, that a change in social policies may really be what is needed (Anyon 2005). They understand that sometimes schools are a community's only lifeline, because other social supports have already been retracted (Tuck 2012). Your school leaders respond to this social reality with an ethic of abundance, not scarcity. They ensure that all students have hot food, clean and warm clothing, and books to read. When students do not have these things, the school provides them. No one is considered undeserving.

Your school leaders and teachers have a vision for your shared work in school. They know that everything they teach you must have a present and a future purpose. Your school leaders and teachers understand that schooling must be about more than getting into college, getting a "good" job, or acquiring a piece of property. **Your teachers understand that your schooling is more than cramming your head full of government-approved curriculum. They teach you how to draw your own conclusions based on facts you have been presented with, conversations you have with your peers and educators, and your own unique background and life experiences. Your teachers are not bank tellers, doling out information as if it were a series of dollar bills.**

Schooling involves a whole community in which teachers and students are comfortable discussing issues pertinent to the world around them. Your school helps students go gracefully into the world prepared to work for what they believe will fulfill their goals and create the change they find most compelling. You and your peers will be taught not to internalize the morality of your teachers and institutions but rather to develop and understand a morality of your own so that you may endeavor to live by a code of ethics in harmony with your own thinking.

The Work of Teaching

Your teachers have enough time to plan your interaction with them and envision the arc of your learning. They know how to plan, and they do so using open online platforms — documents, online bulletin boards, and other collaborative tools — to plan and collaborate with colleagues and share with families and school leaders. **Instead of leading you through a predetermined curriculum, your teachers will help you cultivate your own vision in a social context. Where you may see little, your teachers will see the seeds of potential: a potential in you and a potential in our community. In helping you to enact your vision, your teachers will act as networkers, recruiting parents and community members to join this partnership. Your teachers are also consultants, providing you with essential information, and allies, encouraging you and working alongside you toward your vision. Working with your teachers, you will organize your vision into a series of measured objectives. This will not only impress upon you a model for making change in your world but will also ensure that your academic success is assessed by meaningful measures that you have had a hand in constructing.**

As a result of this effort, tendrils of connectedness will spread and take root, so our community can blossom outward from the walls of the classroom. Together with your teachers and peers, you will establish your own moral anchors and routes of being. Your teachers will prune their lessons and cultivate knowledge in their field. What our oppressors once saw as a vacant lot will soon produce fruit. When they discover what produced this harvest they will try to destroy it, but they will find the roots too thick to crack and the soil too sweet to spoil with acids and weeds. You'll quickly discover that cooperative toil accrues purpose and value. You will learn something unique about life: it can be fostered from every plot.

Teacher Education

Your teachers are trusted and trustworthy. They have spent years getting ready to work with you, learning and teaching alongside mentor teachers along the way. Your teachers receive regular sabbatical opportunities to return to graduate school or participate in other sustained professional development. They too are lifelong learners, always making space for new and reclaimed practices, continually reflecting and imagining the future. **Every teacher has been a student first. All of your teachers have also had teachers who shaped them and made them who they are today. The knowledge they acquired in their teacher education programs has made them aware of issues in education as well as social justice.**

Your teachers have learned extensive methods and practices for making their classrooms effective and engaging. This education has given them the foundation to make your classroom your intellectual and emotional home. Even with a certification to teach, they still continue to learn. The best teachers are beacons of hope. Your teachers work to better themselves both inside and outside the classroom, because the more they learn, the more they can share with you. Your teachers understand that it is not their job to change you but rather to show you that you are capable of changing yourself. Your teachers all entered the teaching profession because they had a passion. You may not have that same passion, but you will use their excitement and energy to find your own calling.

References

Anyon, Jean. 2005. *Radical Possibilities: Public Policy, Urban Education, and a New Social Movement.* New York: Routledge.

Tuck, Eve. 2012. *Urban Youth and School Pushout: Gateways, Get-aways, and the GED.* New York: Routledge.

Eve Tuck, *PhD, teaches courses in Educational Studies and Native American Studies at the State University of New York at New Paltz. Her writings focus on the lived experiences of education policies, the ethics of social science research, settler colonialism, and youth participatory action research. She is the author of* Urban Youth and School Pushout: Gateways, Getaways, and the GED *(2012), co-editor of* Youth Resistance and Theories of Change *(2014), and co-author of* Place in Research: Theory, Methodology, and Methods *(2014). Eve's co-authors in this essay are graduate students in a Social Foundations of Education course, offered at SUNY New Paltz.*

An Exercise in Challenging Teachers' Assumptions About the Way Schools Are

Sonia Nieto

I've taught preservice and practicing teachers for nearly thirty years on topics ranging from multicultural education, curriculum development, bilingual education, and the education of Puerto Rican students, among others. One of the primary goals of my courses was to ask students to examine the reality of public schools, as opposed to the common myths many of us carry around: schools as the "great equalizer," schools as serving an unquestioned meritocracy, schools as a level playing field. These are all good and noble myths, but myths nevertheless, and any serious look into how schools work, who benefits, who gets ahead and why, will disabuse people of the veracity of these myths (Spring 2012). They are, however, noble ideals and aspirations toward which we, as educators and as a society, should strive.

To help students — both undergraduate and graduate — become aware of the grim realities of inequality, while at the same time maintaining their hope that the situation might be otherwise, is a tremendous challenge, one that I accepted from the time I became a teacher educator. It was not an easy task. To do so, I had to come up with creative ways to help students develop what Paulo Freire (1970) called *conscientização* — a critical consciousness about education in particular, and society in general.

In the courses I taught, my students (most of whom were preservice and practicing teachers) not only read books and articles, but also kept journals, watched videos, participated in simulations, engaged in group work, prepared debates, listened to speakers, did presentations on sundry contentious issues in education, and took part in other activities that I hoped would challenge their taken-for-granted assumptions about public education. One activity in particular — to design the "ideal" school — seemed especially appropriate for this book on imagining schools as they should be.

Designing an Ideal School

For this activity, I was especially interested in the goals my students thought schools should attempt to accomplish, that is, I wanted them to grapple with the age-old question, *What is the purpose of education?* This activity took place near the end of the semester, after they had already delved into a number of consequential topics including the nature of pluralism and intergroup relations in US schools and society; the causes and consequences of the complex dynamics of racism, sexism, and other forms of individual and institutional discrimination; and the historical and contemporary experiences of various cultural groups in US society, particularly in education. The focus of the unit on which this activity was based was to analyze the influence of learning on such sociocultural and sociopolitical variables as race, ethnicity, gender, and social class background, among others; and to gain an understanding of how the institutional structures, policies, and practices of schools tend to perpetuate discriminatory inequities by their effects on students and educators. It was during this unit, specifically the second part of the objective, that this activity took place.

To ascertain whether the students had understood, in a concrete way, how particular school-based policies and practices affect the schooling of students of different social, cultural, racial, linguistic, ability, and socioeconomic background, I asked them to get into one of four groups. Each group received a card that had a stated purpose of education. These were:

1. To create many low-skilled workers and a few highly skilled managers

2. To replicate society

3. To prepare students for lives as productive citizens of a democratic society

4. To prepare students to live peacefully and equitably in a multicultural society.

My students' job was to design "ideal" schools, each of which would embody one of these goals. Specifically, I asked them to keep in mind the school's policies and practices including curriculum, pedagogy, assessment, tracking, family outreach, hiring, professional development, and so on. How would these policies and practices define the goal of this school? How would the goal be evident as soon as one stepped into the school?

This was a "fun" activity that students typically enjoyed. They came up with all manner of creative and unique schools, although I noticed that it was often not until we had discussed their "ideal" school in more depth that they made the connection between how schools are organized and what they are meant to accomplish.

For the first "ideal" school (to create many low-skilled workers and a few highly skilled managers), there was no shortage of rigid and punitive practices and policies in place. For example, my students envisioned schools where young people were tracked from kindergarten through high school based on an initial assessment that followed them throughout their schooling. As a result, only a few privileged students were permitted to take advanced courses by the time they reached high school. The curriculum differed dramatically, with most students taking classes that would, for the most part, teach them practical skills, and a few taking classes that would help them develop leadership abilities. The privileged were treated to an arts-rich curriculum, while all others were given only a rudimentary and utilitarian curriculum that focused on basic skills: no art, no music, no physical education. Families of privileged students would be welcomed into the school with open arms, and they would have free rein over decision making concerning the curriculum and instruction, while less privileged parents, as well as teachers, would have very little say in selecting or creating curriculum or in using innovative pedagogical strategies.

The goal of the second "ideal" school (to replicate society) resulted in even more dehumanizing policies and practices. This kind of school was organized according to the "haves" and the "have-nots," in terms of social class, race, native language, and so on. As a result, students were grouped according to their race, ethnicity, social class, and level of proficiency in English. In addition, students with disabilities were completely segregated from their peers in basement classrooms and, as a result, they were never able to interact with other students. New, inexperienced teachers were assigned to work with the "have-nots," while better, more experienced teachers taught the privileged students. The curriculum reflected these prejudices: privileged students were exposed to interesting, mind-expanding curricula and exciting pedagogy, while the unprivileged learned a rudimentary worksheet-based curriculum through rote memorization. Sometimes, the students imagining this "ideal" school would even have two separate but connected schools, one with many resources and the other resource-poor.

The third and fourth "ideal" schools, not surprisingly, turned out to be much more humanistic, inclusive, and equitable. Students in the third "ideal" school (to prepare students for lives as productive citizens of a democratic society), for instance, had access to a curriculum that included lessons involving a critical analysis of history, along with the practical skills needed for productive participation in a democratic society. There were elections and student councils that met regularly with teachers and administrators to make school-policy decisions. Parents were also encouraged to participate in these decisions. In the fourth "ideal" school (to prepare students to live peacefully and equitably in a multicultural society), the curriculum and pedagogy were multicultural and culturally responsive to the student body. Students were encouraged to speak their native language and, where the numbers allowed, bilingual or even trilingual classes were provided. Teachers were also given the opportunity to study other languages as part of their professional development.

In both the third and fourth "ideal" schools, teachers were given time, attention, and resources to develop their craft. In both kinds of schools, community engagement projects were not only encouraged, they were required as a significant component of the curriculum. In addition, the arts and physical education were incorporated into every school day.

Reflections

As is apparent from the brief description I've given, the first two types of schools were uncannily similar to our current public schools, while the third and fourth schools were utopian and visionary places. I think that, without always fully realizing it, with the first two imagined schools my students had recreated the schools with which they were familiar. These also turned out to be places in which they would not want to work. Why this happened time and again can be explained by the fact that we don't always question that which is familiar to us, even when it's negative or detrimental. This is the case of the two schools that represented the status quo.

When given alternative models, however, we come to realize what is wrong with what we know. The last two schools, on the other hand, represented the best of my students' imagination, creativity, and vision for what schools should be. In our discussions after the activity, we often marveled at the tremendous chasm between our society's stated ideals of "equal and equitable education" and the reality of our actual schools, particularly for our most vulnerable students. How is it that we proclaim one thing and yet end up with another? How is it possible that we have so many schools that are segregated, unequal, unimaginative, rigid, and unhealthy — emotionally and in other ways — for children? I remember one of my students saying, "Maybe we have the schools we deserve," because, as she said, "we know what schools should be and yet a majority of schools are so different from what we profess." It gave us food for thought. It also made us think about Lisa Delpit's (1988) reflections on how what we want for our own children sometimes differs markedly from what we think "other people's children" deserve.

It took an exercise like this for preservice and practicing teachers to reflect critically on how power is implicated in all decisions concerning education, whether curriculum, testing, tracking, retention, pedagogy, or other factors. These decisions do not fall out of the sky, nor are they based on any particular logic or order. Rather, they are generally based on who has power and how it is used. The result is that some students experience safe, engaging, and fulfilling schools, while other children — sometimes in the same town or city but in decidedly different neighborhoods — experience schools that are lifeless, boring, and disrespectful; schools that are harmful to both students and teachers. Mary Poplin and Joseph Weeres (1992), in extensive research with students, teachers, and others inside schools, captured this sentiment in the words of a student who described his school by saying, "This school hurts my spirit" (11). We need to ask: *How many students' (and teachers') spirits are hurt by the kinds of schools they attend?*

This exercise also spurred teachers to question their taken-for-granted assumptions about schools and, more importantly, got them to think about what they could do — as classroom teachers, as members of school communities and professional organizations, and as citizens of their town or city — to initiate change and help schools become more in line with the kind of education we say we stand for. Each time I did the activity, I was also reminded that no lofty ideal is worth its salt if it rarely gets realized. This is particularly true of public education, which is, after all, our best hope for creating a society that is truly democratic, equitable, and free.

References

Delpit, Lisa. 1988. "The Silenced Dialogue: Power and Pedagogy in Educating Other People's Children." *Harvard Educational Review* 58 (3): 280–298.

Freire, Paulo. 1970. *Pedagogy of the Oppressed.* New York: Seabury Press.

Poplin, Mary, and Joseph Weeres. 1992. "Voices From the Inside: A Report on Schooling from Inside the Classroom." Claremont, CA: The Institute for Education in Transformation, Claremont Graduate School.

Spring, Joel. 2012. *Deculturalization and the Struggle for Equality: A Brief History of the Education of Dominated Cultures in the United States,* Seventh edition. New York: McGraw-Hill.

*Educator, researcher, writer, and teacher, **Sonia Nieto** is Professor Emerita of Language, Literacy, and Culture at the School of Education, University of Massachusetts, Amherst. In her career, Sonia has taught students from elementary school through doctoral studies, and her research has focused on multicultural education, teacher education, and the education of Latinos, immigrants, and other students of culturally and linguistically diverse backgrounds.*

Progressive Education as Liberation

(or, *Is Public Education for Someone Else's Children?*)

Sayantani DasGupta

Where the mind is without fear and the head is held high
Where knowledge is free

— Rabindranath Tagore

I believe in the connections between education and liberation. Not just who can be educated, but what they learn and how we teachers educate, are all issues of social justice. As a professor of Narrative Medicine — an interdisciplinary medical humanities field that seeks to honor the role of storytelling in health care — my own seminar-style teaching is deeply influenced by thinkers like Paulo Freire and bell hooks. I seek to teach courses such as "Narrative, Health, and Social Justice" in a way that is consistent with my course content. People-first, anti-oppression work can't be taught from a position of hierarchy and didactic pedagogy. There must be a different paradigm, whereby professors see themselves as problem posers and members — rather than leaders — of classroom communities. In such a model, education is not the purview of the elite; it is a tool of people's freedom.

Yet I haven't been able to easily find such an educational model for my own children, or yours. A daughter of immigrants, educated in the US public school system, I did not choose a public education for my children. Rather than hide it, I want to spend some time talking about a choice that's flawed and more than personal, in hopes that we can use the information for positive collective action.

For my children, I chose a progressive, independent (pre)K–8 school that values nurturing and free play, art and music, intellectual curiosity, and social community. I wanted an alternative to what I saw happening in US public schools: slashed art and music budgets, reduced recess, inordinate time spent on class discipline, and relentless test preparation. No Child Left Behind, Race to the Top, high-stakes testing, and more recently, the Common Core, have all been effective creators of high-pressure, high-compliance environments, not of innovative children. I resist such environments because I know how powerful they can be.

During the struggle for Indian independence from two hundred years of British rule, my paternal grandfather earned a doctorate in education and eventually became principal of Kolkata's Teacher's Training College. Growing up, my father would often regale me with stories of a childhood spent going from progressive school to progressive school — many of which were in fact set up by my grandparents with my father's best interests in mind. I cannot think that my grandparents' feelings about progressive education were disconnected from their passion regarding India's struggle for freedom from her colonialist masters. Indeed, as the direction of a free India was to be guided by the hearts and minds of her citizens, rather than by a distant ruler, the schools my grandparents founded met their students' needs rather than expecting the students to meet the schools' imposed requirements. My father, a scientist by training, often waxes poetic about these free schools based on self-directed learning, where he was seen and valued as a holistic human being, not simply as a widget in an educational machine.

And yet, even when we see all that can come from such a progressive model, a lot of the impetus for educational reform feels based on the fear of "someone else's children." A focus on rules and obedience in US schools undoubtedly has racialized origins. For some, compliance feels safer than what we can't predict. In addition, our current public education model, informed by high-stakes testing, reflects what Freire called the "banking model of education," whereby students' heads are metaphorically opened and knowledge poured in. It's a model in which the teacher knows everything and the students know nothing, the teacher acts and the students are acted upon, the teacher is the subject of the learning process while the pupils are mere objects. At the risk of being accused of hyperbole, such models can be likened to a sort of "educational colonialism" — a ruling of the uninformed masses from an all-knowing, yet distant, set of masters.

The racial politics evident in such policies extend themselves beyond US borders when we justify educational reforms by declaring that "we" are "falling behind" India, China, and other countries. Such concerns not only ignore the fact that "we" are made up of plenty of Indian, Chinese, and other immigrants, but also forget that the United States is still the world leader in technological innovation. (One could argue that it's also about being uncomfortable with the changing nature of "we," but that's another essay.)

Innovative thinking is about flexibility, not rote memorization or excessive standardized test-taking. Indeed, in Silicon Valley, an arguable bastion of technological innovation, many computer executives send their children to a purposefully low-tech Waldorf school (Richtel 2011), a private school that these executives must, of course, pay for. And yet, this gesture is not dissimilar to my own family's choices. Like good teachers everywhere, the Silicon Valley geeks know what policy makers don't; that you can't standardize innovative thinking. You can only nurture individual ways of knowing. Because I wanted this for my child, I chose a private progressive school, first for preschool, and then kindergarten, then first grade; always thinking "this is the last year, and then we go to public school," never guessing that I would put my second child in that school as well.

My field, Narrative Medicine, or medical humanities, is a clinical and scholarly movement to honor the relationship that is at the heart of healthcare. Its purpose is to recognize that healing is an intersubjective, human experience, as well as a scientific one. Freire taught us that education can, and must, be a tool of liberation, which respects the knowledge that learners bring to the classroom and models a power-sharing between learner and educator that can be taken out of the classroom and into the community (Freire 2000). In bringing literature, philosophy, art, music, cultural studies, oral history, and the like to the healthcare classroom, Narrative Medicine values multiple ways of knowing — the scientific and the storied, the medical and the artistic — despite the resistance we get from our humanities colleagues who resent the "real world" justifications of liberal arts, and our scientific colleagues who look down upon anything but quantifiable ways of knowing. It is also a movement aimed at addressing medical hierarchy and translating a sense of narrative humility (Das-Gupta 2008, 2013) from the classroom to the clinic room, thereby changing medical culture itself.

How can we similarly change the culture of public school education? In the words of a poet and educator who was central to India's independence, perhaps what we seek is:

> *Where the mind is without fear and the head is held high*
> *Where knowledge is free*
> *Where the world has not been broken up into fragments*
> *By narrow domestic walls*
> *Where words come out from the depth of truth*
> *Where tireless striving stretches its arms towards perfection*
> *Where the clear stream of reason has not lost its way*
> *Into the dreary desert sand of dead habit*
> *Where the mind is led forward by thee*
> *Into ever-widening thought and action*
> *Into that heaven of freedom, my Father, let my country awake.*

> —"Where the Mind Is Without Fear," Rabindranath Tagore

The poet Tagore not only penned songs and poems with deeply revolutionary themes, but when he established Visva-Bharati University in Santiniketan in 1921, his goal was that the university be a meeting place for (a then British-occupied) India and the world. The methodology of teaching in the university, and the accompanying school, made central the bodies of learners and the body of the Indian nation itself, rather than looking Westward for educational methodology and content. Tagore's choice to establish outdoor classrooms where students and teachers could learn, weather permitting, in the natural environment, stemmed from his reservations about the British-imposed systems of Western education. He felt, in fact, that any teaching done within four walls represented a limitation of the mind and spirit. Indeed, Tagore's words seem to echo Freire's "banking model of education": "education consists in the training of all the senses, along with the mind instead of cramming the brain with memorized knowledge" (Kripalani 1962, p. 8). Giving learners a sense of themselves in the environment and the world was a central part of his educational vision. In his essay "A Poet's School," Tagore describes a childhood trip with his father to the Himalayas at age ten, where he was allowed to roam free in nature. He says the "founding of my school had its origin in the memory of that longing for freedom, the memory which seems to go back beyond the sky-line of my birth" (Tagore 1997, p. 253).

What would this sort of "place-based education" (Smith and Sobel 2010) look like in the United States today? Certainly, in an age of risk aversion and helicopter parenting, environmental degradation and climate change, children need to learn how to care for the world around them. They need to understand themselves as citizens of their neighborhoods, their nation, and their planet. Yet, at a time where the gap between the rich and the poor is only escalating, progressive education visions are really only accessible to a small group of privileged children in the United States. Notable exceptions are innovative, environmentally conscious movements, such as "edible schoolyard" programs, which partner with public schools to build gardens and kitchen classrooms (Waters 2008). Public education is increasingly shaped by numbers and regulations, whereby children are being molded to fit the educational curricula, rather than the curricula being shaped by children's unique needs, talents, and curiosities.

Educator and activist bell hooks writes that the act of teaching itself can be a tool of transgression. In her words, "I entered the classroom with the conviction that it was crucial for me and every other student to be an active participant, not a passive consumer. . . . Education as the practice of freedom . . . education that connects the will to know with the will to become. Learning is a place where paradise can be created" (hooks 1994).

Let us not be afraid to imagine these innovative connections in US public schools: progressive, student-centered education that values our learners' spirits and voices more than merely evaluating their deficits. Our children — all of our children — hold the entire world in their hands. Let us give them the strength and gentleness to hold it well.

References

DasGupta, Sayantani. 2008. "Narrative humility." *The Lancet.* 371 (9617): 980–981.

———. 2013. "Narrative humility." *TEDxSLC talk.* www.tedxtalks.ted.com/video/Narrative-Humility-Sayantani-Da.

Freire, Paulo. 2000. *Pedagogy of the Oppressed,* 30th Anniversary Edition. New York: Continuum.

hooks, bell. 1994. *Teaching to Transgress: Education as the Practice of Freedom.* New York: Routledge.

Kripalani, Krishna. 1962. *Rabindranath Tagore: A Biography.* New York: Grove Press.

Richtel, Matt. 2011. "A Silicon Valley School That Doesn't Compute." *New York Times.* October 22. http://www.nytimes.com/2011/10/23/technology/at-waldorf-school-in-silicon-valley-technology-can-wait.html

Smith, Gregory. A., and David. Sobel. 2010. *Place- and Community-Based Education in Schools.* New York: Routledge.

Tagore, Rabindranath. 1997. "A Poet's School." In K. Dutta K. and A. Robinson (eds.), *Rabindranath Tagore: An Anthology* (pp. 248–261). London: Picador.

———. 1962. *Gitanjali.* New York: St. Martin's Press.

Waters, Alice. 2008. *Edible Schoolyard: A Universal Idea.* New York: Chronicle Books.

**Sayantani DasGupta**, *MD, MPH, is faculty in the Master's Program in Narrative Medicine, co-chair of the University Seminar in Narrative, Health, and Social Justice, and faculty fellow in the Center for the Study of Social Difference, all at Columbia University. She also teaches in the Graduate Program in Health Advocacy at Sarah Lawrence College. She is the author of a memoir, co-author of a book of folktales, and co-editor of an award-winning collection of women's illness narratives* Stories of Illness and Healing: Women Write Their Bodies. *Her creative and academic work has been widely anthologized and published in venues including* Ms. Magazine, *The JAMA Network,* the Hastings Center Report, *and* The Feminist Wire. *She is the mother of a daughter and a son.*

PART **2**

Imagine Instruction That Engages and Changes Students

The Public School System as Resistance to Corporate Power and Control

An Interview with Noam Chomsky

Luke Reynolds

Do you think test scores and grades help students to be motivated?

Grades, scores, etc., are all forced. That's all force, not motivation. If you think about kids when they're little, you get a pretty good picture of motivation. The main thing a kid will ask his parents is *Why?* Now that's not just to keep the conversation going; kids are naturally inquisitive, they want to know what's happening, what's going on, and why. That goes on all the way to graduate school. I work at a major institution, and many people here — they're not working because of force, but because of interest.

You've articulated two routes for public education in America: indoctrination or discovery. Can you share a little about what education as discovery would look like in our public schools?

You can run classes in such a way that children explore, create, and come to understand — not just memorize. I have a friend who teaches sixth grade, and she told me how she was teaching a section on the American Revolution. One way to do it is just to applaud the courage of George Washington and so on. But how she taught it was a little different; she began by imposing arbitrary restrictions on her students, and they began to resent it more and more. She imposed more restrictions, and her students got fed up. At that point she introduced their study of the American Revolution and said, *OK, this is why people rebel.* You can learn something about yourself in this. We can all learn about ourselves by what we experience and by what we engage with.

There's another example portrayed in the major science magazines of the country. A major complaint is that science is being carried out in dull ways, without any recognition of the fun and discovery within it. As an example of what's possible, in a kindergarten class, each child was given a dish with objects in it — pebbles, shells, beads, seeds — and the task was for each child to figure out which ones were seeds. First, they had a scientific conference and they discussed how to go about exploring each object in their dishes, and they discussed how they might come to figure out which of them were seeds. Then, the students experimented. Finally, they were given magnifying glasses, and they broke open the objects and looked inside. These kids learned something about open inquiry, and this can be done at any level. It's very different from teaching to the test and evaluating teachers based only on student test scores. The students didn't memorize anything, but they learned a great deal more than they would if they had been preparing for a test.

How do you view the current trends in privatization and market-based principles in public school reform, and what impact do you think they're having on teachers and students?

I don't like to use the word *reform*, which has a positive connotation with it. When Maoist China induced change, we didn't call it reform. We called it change. One of the great achievements of the United States was engineering public mass education, and that it went from schools to colleges — like land-grant colleges. Right now, I'm sitting in what began as a land-grant college [Massachusetts Institute of Technology]. The mass public education system was a major achievement, and there have been efforts to destroy it for a long time from powerful sectors. Corporate entities can't control it. They want to find ways to control it and overcome it, but it has resisted. Currently, though, that's where the money and funding are — in pressure to control and change the public mass education system so that it can be controlled and serve the elite.

The other, deeper, problem is that the public school system is based on the principles of solidarity and support. So if you really accept the right-wing view that *I shouldn't pay taxes because my kids don't go to school* — well, that's simply pathological. The public school system is based on the idea that we *do* care about other people. That's what it comes down to. Charter schools undermine public schools, and the other problem is that schools are very much underfunded. If you want to destroy a system, underfund it and then people will say we've got to privatize it. As an example, when Margaret Thatcher wanted to destroy the public railroad system in Britain, she underfunded it, and then she privatized it. That's what is happening with American schools now.

There are other concerns, too. The United States is certainly unique in the way public schools are funded. Around the country, schools are funded by property taxes. In any community, historically, there could be a mix of rich and poor, so you had some fairly decent funding. I don't want to euphemize it, but historically communities tended to have more of a mix of wealth. But now the country is much more segregated by wealth. For instance, in Boston, where I live, in affluent suburbs the schools are well funded, but in poor communities, they're not. Affluent suburbs rob the inner cities in all kinds of ways. For example, when I drive in to Cambridge in the morning, I drive in on the city streets. I'm not paying for the taxes on these city streets because I live in a suburb; the poorer city residents are paying for these streets. The wealthy are robbing the poor. In numerous other ways, this happens.

Another factor is the lack of respect for teachers. One person who has written about this is Diane Ravitch. She points out that if you go to countries with fairly effective education systems, teaching is a more highly respected profession. But in the United States, the teaching profession is treated without respect. My wife, when she taught at the Harvard Graduate School of Education, went to international conferences, and she often noticed this too. Teachers overseas were treated with dignity and value — they were highly respected. People want dignity and respect.

Do you think there are ways to stop these current trends?

Sure: public action. I give hundreds of talks, and I've noticed over the past couple of years that I've been asked to give more and more talks on public education. For example, I recently gave talks in Harlem and in the Mississippi Delta. Both were community talks, and one of the things people are concerned about is the undermining of the public education system. They understand it well and they want it to stop.

 **Noam Chomsky** *has lectured at many universities, here and abroad, and is the recipient of numerous honorary degrees and awards. He has written and lectured widely on linguistics, philosophy, intellectual history, contemporary issues, international affairs, and U.S. foreign policy. Among his more recent books are,* New Horizons in the Study of Language and Mind; On Nature and Language; The Essential Chomsky; Hopes and Prospects; Gaza in Crisis; How the World Works; 9–11: Was There an Alternative?; Making the Future: Occupations, Interventions, Empire and Resistance; The Science of Language; Peace with Justice: Noam Chomsky in Australia; Power Systems; *and* On Western Terrorism: From Hiroshima to Drone Warfare *(with Andre Vltchek).*

Teachers Making Change

Steven Zemelman

Change is good. You go first.

— Marny Daniels

Building democracy, engagement, and authentic inquiry in the complex, hierarchical organizations we call schools is not a simple thing. Can they promote resistance to corporate power in America? That would be a great gift, since we would not just achieve change but would grow a whole new generation of citizens committed to it. Certainly, there is a small minority of smart, savvy educators who do this very actively now. And teachers who quietly help kids become thoughtful, critical thinkers also helps. But I would argue that schools first need to become more democratic within themselves if they are ever to be a real force for change. So what can we learn from the struggles of teachers who have indeed promoted critical engagement to help us achieve such learning for all children in the future?

Scene: I'm visiting a wonderful seventh-grade math class taught by Dorne Eastwood. The kids are writing in math journals so they get to think about what they're doing *before* they complete the problems they're trying to solve. I interview several of the kids, and here's one exchange:

ME: Have you ever had a math journal before this year?

STUDENT: No, never.

ME: Do you like it?

STUDENT: Sure!

ME: Why? How does it help you?

STUDENT: It really helps me think for myself. When the teacher explains the problem later, I get to compare how I thought about it with how she does it. That way if I had any trouble I can understand why. So I get to learn more on my own.

But Dorne is completely alone doing such work at this school. The principal is autocratic and uninterested in instruction. Teachers don't get opportunities to collaborate. Ultimately Dorne leaves for another teaching job that isn't so isolating.

Reflection: A great many teachers do wonderful things with kids. Some are lucky enough to be in schools where colleagues share strategies, connect student growth and community across grade levels, and contribute to their school's leadership. Others are quite alone in their work. Powerful teaching and learning may actually be happening in other classrooms, but individual teachers don't necessarily know about it. It's an egg-crate approach to school organization. **For a future with great schools, we need not only inspiring and empowering classrooms but mutually supportive communities of teachers. Educators must share leadership, responsibility, and ideas widely.**

Scene: I visit a school to observe and evaluate the work of an outstanding consultant who is helping to implement student-centered teaching strategies. I interview a group of newer teachers who love the ideas but are actually miserable, snubbed by the more experienced teachers who feel threatened by the changes being pressed on them. Later in the year, the older group of teachers is able to influence the local school council (Chicago schools are guided, to some extent, by these) to fire the innovative new principal. Improvement project over. Subsequently, many of the newer teachers leave.

Postscript: Several years later, I visited the same school for a different project, and the current principal told me, "A lot of healing was needed here." One of her strategies was to meet regularly with each teacher, listen to his or her concerns, and look for ways to address them. Later, one of the "old guard" teachers approached me to brag about a new strategy that was working with her students.

Reflection: So wait a minute. Such exciting ways for kids to learn were being introduced. How could things have gone so wrong? And what magic helped to straighten them out later? Reading Charles Payne's insightful but depressing *So Much Reform, So Little Change* helps us understand. The principal and consultant were thinking progressively about classrooms but not very smartly about the *social dynamic* among the adults in the school. Just mandate everyone to adopt the new strategies? That approach mainly exacerbated factions among the teachers and ultimately undermined their efforts. So I began to wonder if perhaps a lot of the work we'd been doing in the Illinois Writing Project (that I direct) had also not been very smart. There's a contradiction when "democratic" classroom strategies are being *forced* on teachers. While we hadn't been the enforcers, per se, working only with the "eager and willing" sometimes unwittingly supported them. So the question becomes how to promote educational improvement and democracy within a hierarchical — and sometimes fragile — organization? The subsequent principal, who met with all the teachers and worked on at least some of their concerns, had learned a key strategy that some of us had begun to pick up from community organizers. **The implication for achieving a future with great schools? Democratic methods, by definition, can't be forced on people. First, we need to build relationships, trust, and respect. Next, develop structure and practices through which everyone can contribute from their strengths. Then build a professional culture in which people listen to each other, learn from each other, and allow for differences while sharing mutual responsibility. A tall order, yes, but we've seen these things done.**

Scene: It's 8:15 a.m. and I'm sitting with a school's instructional leadership team, made up almost entirely of teachers representing the various grade-levels and subject areas. They're working to promote writing workshops in every classroom and are reviewing their progress and next efforts. In writing workshops, students spend class time on their own choices of topics, while the teacher helps individuals with specific needs. Students also share their writing with the class so they have a real audience for their words.

The team has broken the development process into small, doable steps, starting simply with the physical classroom arrangement that can support the various stages of students' work. The team members have communicated regularly with all the teachers and responded to their concerns. Now they're working to help teachers design effective mini-lessons that come at the beginning of each workshop session. The principal marvels afterward, "I could never have come up with these ideas for making this project work." The school's scores on the state *reading* tests jump 46 points that year — an accomplishment, even if you don't believe in the validity of the tests.

Postscript: Several years later a new principal took over, a much less secure or confident leader, who promptly disbanded the leadership team.

Reflection: Hooray, but also ouch! So a more successful, democratic structure was taking root, but the school remained vulnerable to organizational changes that could too easily dial that back. Distributed, democratic leadership can be powerful, but it isn't yet shared widely enough among educators to enable sustainability or spread. Research by Andy Hargreaves and Dean Fink has shown how progressive schools can slip backward over time, though these smart educators also offer strategies for preventing that from happening. Fortunately, in every school where such powerful growth takes place, students and teachers gain a vision of what meaningful, democratic, and effective education can look like. These classroom strategies and leadership structures keep popping up over and over. No amount of restrictive bureaucratic control can keep them from reemerging and gaining new strength and expertise each time they reappear. **Lesson for the future of education: Lasting**

change in schools will require a widespread cultural shift. We will all need to learn to balance distributed leadership and guidance within democratic institutions.

Further, shared leadership and support for student efficacy and community don't necessarily develop automatically, especially when teachers and school leaders haven't had much experience of them. For productive sharing of powerful ideas about teaching and learning, an effective democratic institution requires well-organized but open structures and training to use them well. The teachers on that team had no previous experience working together or guiding school-wide change. They received in-depth training sessions and an external coach to help them learn to lead meetings, settle disagreements productively, listen to fellow teachers' issues, identify a meaningful and doable educational focus and student outcome, plan an improvement process, build support among fellow teachers, and work to make sure the new instructional strategy gets implemented and is effective. Democracy and self-efficacy for students are not conditions we arrive at. They are processes we must reclaim again and again. **For a future with effective democratic schools: We'll need structures and training in how to use them to enable real, sustainable change within the schools themselves and to serve as an engine for advocacy and change in their communities.**

Scene: It's an intense September Saturday in Chicago. A group of us has organized a TEDx talk event featuring nine Chicago teachers, a student, a principal, and five community leaders, all sharing stories of powerful teaching and learning that have made a difference for kids, and that could help many more if the right policies supported them. One high school social studies teacher, Elizabeth Robbins, recounts how her students identified a significant community problem — in this case, date violence — and researched instructional programs addressing it. They decided none of the programs were good enough, so they designed their own, field-tested it, presented it to the Chicago School Board, and saw it adopted as an official program within the Chicago Public Schools. The kids, of course, came away tremendously empowered. "We don't realize how much our kids can do," Elizabeth reminded us. "Our students are not just the future: they are the NOW" she declared. Her story and others are now available to view on YouTube. You can search "TEDxWellsStreetED" to see them. Ironically, when you type this in the search box, it will try to reinterpret your request as a search for *Wall Street*! But don't let it fool you.

Reflection: There are possibilities inside schools, but they can only blossom with support from the rest of the community around them. So many outstanding teachers make a tremendous difference for their students. So many efforts flower, like those of the math and social studies teachers and the instructional leadership team we observed. But so little of the public knows about this — about the exhilarating, difficult, patient, inventive, caring, skillful, exhausting work that good teachers do — and this lack of awareness allows for a destructive narrative about public education to thrive, unanswered. Speaking out has not been part of most American teachers' repertoire, except when we complain in the teachers' lounge or with our life partners. But while many are not ready to risk their jobs complaining about the attacks on public education or the conditions many of us work under, we *can* learn to tell our stories in vivid ways that our fellow citizens can understand. **Lesson for the future: Inequity thrives on lack of awareness. We must tell our stories. Change starts here.**

References

Hargreaves, Andy, and Dean Fink. 2006. *Sustainable Leadership*. San Francisco, CA: Jossey-Bass.

Payne, Charles. 2008. *So Much Reform, So Little Change: The Persistence of Failure in Urban Schools.* Cambridge, MA: Harvard Education Press.

Robbins, Elizabeth. 2013. "Young People Are the NOW." www.TEDxWellsStreetED.com and www.youtube.com.

Steven Zemelman *has helped to develop innovative schools in Chicago and student-centered literacy instruction across the country. He founded and directed the Center for City Schools at National-Louis University and is founding director of the Illinois Writing Project. He has written numerous professional texts on teaching and teacher leadership with co-author Harvey "Smokey" Daniels and others.*

Imagine Educating a Generation of Solutionaries

Zoe Weil

The Purpose of Schooling

As I write this, the current mission of the US Department of Education is "to promote student achievement and preparation for global competitiveness by fostering educational excellence and ensuring equal access."

Is this the mission you want for your school or classroom?

While there's nothing wrong with being prepared for global competitiveness, I believe that this mission is both vague and limited, even myopic, especially in today's world. What's so special about today's world? Only in recent history have we had the capacity to alter the climate of our planet; to cause the extinction of so many species so quickly, threatening biological diversity; to desertify our land and cause dead zones in our oceans, and to potentially bequeath a nuclear winter to the coming generations of all species on Earth. At this very moment, approximately one billion people do not have enough food to eat or clean water to drink, and around twenty-five million people are living as slaves. And this year, close to one trillion animals will be killed for food in ways that are not only unsustainable but are also profoundly inhumane.

Despite this gloomy reality, only in recent history have we also had the capacity to communicate and collaborate instantaneously with people across every border, to work together to solve our challenges, and to create humane, peaceful, just, and restorative systems that benefit all people, all species, and the environment that sustains us. It's exciting to be living at a time when we have such tools for dramatic, cooperative problem solving, and when the information we need to creatively address persistent issues is available through small devices that fit into our pockets. We already have the means and capacities to end poverty, war, oppression, environmental destruction, and so many other global challenges, but we will be hard-pressed to succeed unless we embrace a larger goal for education.

The question, "What is the purpose of schooling?" may be the most important one we can ask at this point in history. The answer will determine whether our graduates will perpetuate (and perhaps escalate) the problems we face, or whether they will have the knowledge, motivation, and tools to solve them.

Imagine what would happen if the guiding questions that children were expected to explore throughout their education and their lives were these:

- What issues in the world most concern you?

- What do you love to do?

- What skills and talents do you have that you could bring to bear on these issues?

- What preparation and knowledge do you need to put your talents and passions to work in order to make a difference and contribute to solutions that will help to create a healthy, humane, and peaceful world?

When we encourage young people to reflect on these fundamental life questions and — over time and throughout their education — find the place where the answers meet, we will help them to live purposefully and to become solutionaries for a healthy future.

Profiles in a Solutionary Education

Six-year-old Darius lies on his stomach in a spring meadow looking at a small square of nature with a magnifying glass. He is staring at tiny hairs on plants and noticing amazing insects—some of who are pollinating flowers. Darius' legs are drying off in the sun after he and his classmates waded wondrously through a vernal pool where they got to see hundreds of frog and salamander eggs.

Even though he lives in a big city, every month Darius' class has been visiting nearby parks where they learn about nature, see and hear wildlife, witness the changes in seasons, taste edible plants, and practice quiet observation.

Darius has spent a good portion of the school year learning to read, and because he loves animals, his teacher has been lending him picture books about nature and wildlife. As he is so excited about these books, they make him even more eager to improve his reading and learn about the natural world on his field trips.

Darius loves his teacher and is sometimes giddy when he gets home; he can't wait to share all the things he has learned.

Every day eleven-year-old Emma wakes up enthusiastic about going to school. All the middle schoolers begin each day spending 10 minutes doing something to make a positive difference. Collectively, that's a week's worth of action—every single morning.

Together, they've written thousands of emails to their legislators; set up new systems for recycling and composting at their school; raised money for charitable organizations by selling note cards with educational messages that they've produced in art class; presented position statements on local issues to their town council; called companies to urge ethical standards in production, and much more.

In various classes, they've worked collaboratively to identify and pursue worthy projects to solve local and global problems; learned how to write and speak respectfully, persuasively, and accurately when reaching out to elected officials and business leaders; explored the local impact of pollution in science class; learned how their math skills can be applied to real-world issues in their community, and gained important academic and life skills every step of the way.

Every once in a while Emma's ideas are chosen as the morning project; she especially loves when that happens. She knows that her voice, her actions, and her hard work matter. Emma knows that she makes a difference each day of her life.

It's fall of Ruby's sophomore year in high school, and she begins each day meeting with her teammates to prepare for their annual county Solutionary Congress, which will be held in the spring. All of the students participate. Ruby's brother's team is focusing on designing a healthy, cost-effective, and humane food system for their school cafeteria, while Ruby's team decided to tackle a massive global issue that has been challenging experts for decades: how to produce and disseminate affordable, clean, renewable energy for a growing population of more than seven billion people.

The multidisciplinary, project-based approach at her school enables Ruby and her brother to study science, math, language arts, social studies, and history with their respective topics in mind. Although Ruby is focused on her own team's ambitious project, she is looking forward to her brother's team's presentation. If her brother's team successfully and persuasively presents their solution, Ruby knows that they might soon have better food choices in the school cafeteria.

If Ruby's team is successful at presenting their ideas, they may get to present at the National Solutionary Congress, during which they'll share their ideas with US senators and representatives, social entrepreneurs, investors, and industry executives. She's never worked so hard in her life as she has on this project — and she's only just started! Ruby finds herself deeply motivated because the project combines both her deep concerns about global climate change and global inequity with her love of science and math. She's already spent hours using online lessons in physics, environmental science, and chemistry, and has loved learning these subjects at her own pace and for her own purposes. At school she's collaborated with her science teacher, who also relishes the opportunity to stretch the curriculum and engage in real-life work with students. Whether Ruby's team's ideas are ultimately adopted or not, she'll know that it is possible to solve big problems.

Leon is an aspiring filmmaker who is passionate about the plight of animals. He spends the spring semester of his senior year interning at an animal sanctuary for rescued farm animals. In consultation with his teachers, the director of the sanctuary, and the local animal control officer, Leon investigates and documents animal cruelty cases. He wants to make a film that will help viewers understand the cruelty inherent in factory farms, and what they can do to stop it.

Leon films his interviews with police officers, legislators, owners of confinement agriculture systems, activists, and the sanctuary staff and its veterinarian. A filmmaking mentor teaches him how to edit his footage. He then crowdsources the funds to produce his movie. Just days after Leon uploads his film to the Internet, it has been viewed ten thousand times. Leon has effectively used his art form to become a successful advocate for voiceless species.

It should be clear from these stories that solutionary education does not require a single sort of school or curriculum. It does, however, require teachers who believe in their students' abilities to contribute to a better world and who provide their students with the information, freedom, opportunities, and capabilities to do so. It also requires a commitment from administrators and educational policy makers to graduate young people who are not only verbally, mathematically, and scientifically literate, but who are ready, willing, and able to apply the knowledge and skills they acquire during their education to make a positive difference in the world, no matter what careers they ultimately pursue.

Our ability to educate such solutionaries depends on teachers fostering students' curiosity, creativity, critical thinking, and collaboration. Teachers need to instill the 3 Rs of reverence, respect, and responsibility, and bring the pressing issues of our time into their classrooms in age-appropriate ways. In this way, our students will understand how to apply what they learn in school toward the goal of doing the most good — and the least harm — to themselves and others in all of their choices, from what they buy, wear, and eat to how they volunteer in their community to how they participate in democracy. Participation in democracy might seem irrelevant to children who can't vote until they are eighteen, but as soon as students write to a legislator in grade school and receive their first response from an elected official, they realize the power of their voice as citizens.

How can teachers educate in such a way that ensures their students have these commitments and capabilities? Through a combination of the following:

- by modeling solutionary thinking and action themselves

- by connecting traditional subject categories to relevant global issues

- by discovering each student's interests and passions

- by paying attention to each students' talents, as well as their challenges; and, to the greatest degree possible, personalizing the curriculum to meet each student's needs and aspirations

- by loving their students and letting them know in every possible way that they matter.

More than any other profession, education determines the future. Will the future be healthy, just, humane, and peaceful? The answer lies largely with what happens every day in classrooms.

 **Zoe Weil** *is the co-founder and President of the Institute for Humane Education: http://humaneeducation.org, which offers online graduate programs, courses, workshops, and free downloadable resources. She's the author of six books, including Nautilus Silver Medal-winner* Most Good, Least Harm; Above All, Be Kind: Raising a Humane Child in Challenging Times; *and* The Power and Promise of Humane Education. *A frequent TEDx speaker, Zoe was honored with Unity College's Women in Environmental Leadership award and was a subject in the Americans Who Tell the Truth portrait series.*

How Can We Educate Diverse Children If Everything Is Standardized?

Allison Skerrett

Student diversity is perhaps the most striking aspect of classrooms in the United States, Canada, and the United Kingdom, nations whose citizens, both immigrant and native born, comprise a mosaic of cultures and languages (Ball et al. 2010; Hargreaves and Skerrett 2012; National Center for Education Statistics 2013). Countries such as Mauritius, Morocco, and St. Martin/St. Maarten, small though they are, also host a multitude of languages, cultures, and national origins (Owodally 2011; Skerrett, under review). The world's nations today are not just multicultural and multilingual; they are also transnational — embracing people who live, work, and learn in two or more countries (Zúñiga and Hamann 2009).

Ironically, in this era of unprecedented student heterogeneity, many educational systems are homogenizing their curricula, instructional language, and assessments (Skerrett and Hargreaves 2008). Pressured by high-stakes accountability, teachers are standardizing their teaching and their learning goals and practices. This further stigmatizes multilingual and multicultural knowledge and abilities in the classroom, and deficit perspectives are becoming more deeply entrenched (Fu and Graff 2009; Martínez-Roldán and Fránquiz 2009).

Between 2010 and 2011, more than 67 percent of students in urban schools came from ethnic backgrounds other than Caucasian, and 15 percent were English language learners. More than 80 percent of city schools served English language learners (National Center for Education Statistics 2013). Already guilty of failing to implement culturally responsive instruction that can build these students' academic literacy and identity (Ladson-Billings 2009), these schools now implement instructional approaches geared only toward passing standardized tests, further dismissing these students' culture and language as resources for teaching and learning.

Teacher educators and teacher candidates also experience this dichotomy between student diversity and educational standardization. I direct an urban teacher preparation program at a large public university. The teacher candidates I work with are eager to draw on students' cultures and language practices in their teaching, but their preservice training takes place in classrooms in which teachers must use scripted daily lesson plans that are tightly linked to "the test." The teacher candidates then see that "learning to teach" involves meekly following an already developed lesson plan.

When teachers are prevented from using our professional expertise to teach uniquely, we must imagine approaches to literacy education that draw on and strengthen our students' existing language and cultural repertoires, while generating new knowledge and abilities necessary for living and learning in diverse societies. With our students, we need to study native language practices and read, write, and analyze multicultural and multilingual texts.

Studying Language Practices

As students from diverse language backgrounds interact with one another, they demonstrate their affiliation with other students that speak their native language; enter new social communities and adopt new identities; navigate local and transnational communities; and strive to attain academic, social, economic, and other rewards (García Sánchez and Orellana 2006; Paris 2011). In particular, they adapt their language to social contexts (Martínez 2010; Skerrett 2012). Let's look at an example.

Vanesa was born in Mexico and began moving between Mexico and the United States when she was twelve. Spanish was her first language, but Vanesa's mother encouraged the family to speak English at home, knowing that fluent English is critical to social, educational, and economic success in the United States. Despite this intention to replace Spanish with English as their primary home language, Spanish remained dominant in Vanesa's home because it was a strong component of their family's cultural identity. As Vanesa put it, "My mom is always telling me that we should speak English all the time, so my little brother can hear us and learn more words and stuff like that. But we usually speak Spanish. Or sometimes we mix the language, but there's more Spanish than English."

Vanesa attended a predominantly white US middle school and was placed in the ELL program. Used to having many school friends in Mexico, during Vanesa's first year in the United States she "just knew like three people that speak Spanish — that's like my basic friends." Gaining greater fluency in English allowed her to expand her friendships to include English-speaking peers: "And then I started talking more English and then I have a lot of friends." English fluency was Vanesa's gateway into social relationships outside her ELL community.

Vanesa then enrolled in a high school whose students were primarily Mexican American and African American. African American English (AAE) was a very different language from the English used by her white middle school peers:

> My middle school was like very white people and here it's like different people and stuff and they speak like another language. Well, not another language, but a slang language and I didn't know those words. People in my other school, like white kids and stuff, they didn't speak like that.

Immersed in a community where AAE and rap music thrived, Vanesa began to appreciate rap and hip-hop:

I started liking it. I don't know why — some words that I just like. And also, like the rappers and stuff, they usually write about their life so I think that's kind of cool, like what you had happen in your life or issues they have, they put it in their song.

In high school, Vanesa also socialized with Mexican American students. In maintaining these friendships she code-switched between English and Spanish: "I text in Spanish with some of my friends but it's weird because we mix the Spanish and English. It's mostly English." When I asked her why she thought she was using English so much more than Spanish, she replied, "I think because I got the language I guess. I don't know. That's weird." She wasn't fully aware that her desire to navigate her life in the United States was shaping her language practices.

If you have many students like Vanesa in your classroom, explicitly studying their language practices is essential to counteract the current standardized approach, which dictates that teachers and students accept the language of the school as the only one that should be discussed, used, and developed in teaching and learning literacy.

Conduct an Inquiry into Students' Language Practice

As a first step, have students keep a journal in which they write about and reflect on all their language practices, at least one entry a day for a week (or however long you feel is appropriate). The following prompt will help them get started:

> Think about the different languages, or the different ways you use language, at home, in school, with friends, and in one or two other situations. Notice how you use language in different spaces and with different people. Why do you think you change your language(s) or ways of speaking?

Broaden the Inquiry into Other Contexts

Assign each student (or pair or small group) the role of ethnographer. Explain that their job is to collect data on the language practices of their families, their social groups, a popular media outlet they enjoy, and the broader community. Data collection approaches that will build students' ability to speak, observe, write, and analyze include:

- conducting and recording interviews

- observing (taking notes, photographs, and making audio or video recordings) how language is used in their various social groups

- identifying significant themes or ideas revealed in these data and thinking about why those are important

- preparing a multimedia report using text, images, audio and video excerpts, and charts or graphs to describe the significant things they learned from their investigations.

Inquire into School Language Practices

Official school practices often contradict and dismiss students' linguistic and cultural practices and identities (Ball et al. 2010). Articulating this mismatch, which many students instinctively feel and notice, is a critical literacy skill. Ask students to observe and take notes on:

- the languages or language practices teachers and students use in classroom conversations

- how teachers and students respond to various languages or language practices in the classroom

- the languages or ways of speaking that are represented in their textbooks, tests, and other learning materials

- how languages and language practices are used in different parts of the school and among different students and school personnel (e.g., how the principal speaks to the students and teachers, how the cafeteria workers speak to the students and the school staff).

Students can then review their observations and reflect, in writing, on what they mean. Students can also keep a reflective journal of how their own languages and language practices are reflected in the academic and social life of the school and how this affects their school experience. Documenting the language used in various areas of their school lives helps students notice and articulate the differing values that may be placed on different languages and their speakers. This also helps students develop their own reasoned moral and political opinions on how language should be acknowledged and used in school.

Share Their Findings

Learning is inherently social, and an individual's learning is enhanced by thinking about and discussing it with others (Vygotsky 1978). Create regular opportunities for students to share their findings on language inquiry. Pair or group culturally and linguistically diverse students, thus encouraging them to notice the ideologies that influence their language practices. Students can share their language journals and discuss their observations and thinking about the language practices of the school or of a particular social context. One member of the pair or group can take notes on intriguing findings or ideas to share with the whole class. Methods of whole-class sharing include:

- language study conferences in which students share longer, multimedia reports

- research roundtables in which three, four, or five students discuss one another's findings

- research posters displaying significant data and findings, including text, images, and other visually appealing elements.

Facilitate Critical Discussion

Critical discussion of the students' language inquiry findings is essential. Model asking critical and collegial questions of a student volunteer who has rehearsed with you beforehand. After the session, have the class discuss the kinds of questions you asked, the purposes behind them, and the kinds of conversations and thinking the questions produced. Then work with a pair or small group of student volunteers and have them share and discuss their research with the class.

These demonstrations help students understand the nature, purposes, and outcomes of sharing and discussing their findings on language use. They can then have those conversations in pairs, small groups, and as a whole class.

Questions that invite critical thinking include:

- What did you learn about how you use language in different spaces and with different people?

- Why do you think you vary your languages or ways of speaking in these different spaces and with these different people?

- Do you ever switch languages or ways of speaking in ways that people you're with don't expect? What happens when you do that?

- What language practices do you use most often? Why do you think that is?

- What did you notice about how different languages are used in different parts of your society? What do those observations suggest to you about the importance, or value, of different languages or language practices in different parts of society?

- What is/are the official language/s of our school? How do you feel about that?

- What is happening to other languages in our school?

- How do you think we can use more of our languages and language practices for learning in our classroom?

Study Language Throughout the Year

Inquiry into language should take place over time, in connection with the rest of your curriculum. Ongoing investigation is necessary because language practices are constantly changing (Orellana and Reynolds 2008; Skerrett 2012). Encourage your students to keep a language journal throughout the year and to write in it at least once every week or two. Have them document and reflect on their own language practices, including whether and when they shift from one language to another. Then create opportunities for students to share their journal entries in class. Have students vary the focus of their study of language practices every few months, and make sure they share important observations or findings. For example, they can create and update a research poster that's displayed in the classroom, or enter and maintain an ongoing research project on a class website. You could also schedule periodic small-group roundtable discussions in which students share what they are learning about language.

Reap the Benefits of Language Study

Studying and discussing language helps students recognize the ideologies embedded in their language practices (Martínez 2010). This will empower you and your students to question and critique the exclusionary language practices of the school and open these practices to all students. Earlier I noted that Vanesa had not reflected consciously or critically on how her language practices had shifted between the dominant languages of her official and unofficial social worlds. Language study helps young people recognize the value of maintaining their original languages while they add new ones and use languages strategically to accomplish personal, social, civic, and academic goals in various social contexts, both in and outside school (New London Group 1996). As students become more aware of language shifts and ideologies, they become more critical, purposeful, and skillful in developing and using their linguistic repertoires.

Reading, Writing, and Analyzing Multicultural and Multilingual Texts

Because literary texts are the foundation of the literacy curriculum, the curricular texts used in diverse classrooms should honor and develop *all* students' cultural and linguistic practices (Ball et al. 2010). This requires that multicultural and multilingual texts be more than alternatives or electives (Lee 2007). Molly, a literacy teacher whose students come from African American, Latina/o, and European American backgrounds, has a classroom library overflowing with teen romances set in urban communities, graphic novels and cartoons connected to the TV shows her students watch, science fiction, and car and sports magazines in English and Spanish. The materials often include AAE and Spanglish. Tales about crossing national borders resonate with many of the students. I once observed Vanesa share a journal entry about a story she was reading: "Vanesa is reading her journal to Nina: something about border crossing, a woman thinking about getting work but she doesn't know what her real job will be" (field notes, March 31, 2010).

The conversations about texts in Molly's classroom incorporate several languages. In the short story "Norma," by Sonia Sanchez, the main character insults a teacher by calling her a hunchback. Molly, knowing this may be an unfamiliar word for both native English and Spanish speakers, asks "How do you even say *hunchback* in Spanish?" and Vanesa helps her with a translation. Carlos, who is from Colombia, often selects books written in Spanish, but he discusses them with both Spanish-speaking and monolingual English students, as well as with Molly. In partnered, small-group, and whole-group interactions, Carlos develops his ability to speak English while maintaining fluency in his home language.

Molly also encourages her students to use all of their linguistic skills in their writing, and her students help one another — and Molly — understand them. For example, after Carlos shares his story written in Spanish, he explains to Nina and Angelica, in Spanish, what his dad was like; Nina and Angelica translate for Molly. Molly says, "He read books to you? No? Oh, you read books to him! Oh, now I'm gonna cry." Molly's objective is to honor and build on her students' cultural and linguistic knowledge and skills, and at the same time help them develop their reading and writing skills in English. Below are some ways you can connect your students' cultural and linguistic practices with the study of literature.

Read and Discuss Texts Written in Many Languages
and Reflective of Many Cultures

Select texts that reflect the languages, cultural practices, and interests of your students. Replace the standard approach (everyone dutifully slogging through the same text as you interpret meaning and facilitate discussion) with flexible reading partnerships, in which the students lead their learning. Certainly, some curricula still mandate that students read specific key texts together, but these texts needn't be their only literary diet. Literature study should also include independent and paired reading, discussion partnerships, and book clubs. Varied reading partnerships are important opportunities for students of both similar and different languages and cultures to read and understand texts together. Partnerships also allow students who share the same interest to develop their knowledge together.

A flexible reading plan might begin like this:

- Start the year, semester, or unit with a short whole-class text (a short story or collection of poems, for example) that contains representations of your students' cultures and languages.

- For a week or two, have students, alone or in pairs, choose texts based on their social, cultural, or linguistic interests or learning needs.

- Introduce and discuss another whole-class text, perhaps one required for your grade level.

- Set up book clubs of four or more students of varied languages and cultures.

If you pay attention to your students' languages and cultures when you choose texts and create student groupings, your class discussions will be more representative of students' linguistic diversity. Encourage students to discuss texts with other students who speak their native language, as well as with students who speak the language they are learning. Students who speak more than one language or dialect often have more highly developed analytic skills in the language or dialect in which they are most fluent (Lee 2007). When you encourage students to use all their languages for reading, thinking, and speaking, they learn a new language more easily.

Discuss Literary Texts Critically

You and your students should also have regular conversations that develop their understanding, appreciation, and appraisal of literature. Help students appreciate the texts that reflect their culture, language, and interests, not just as cool material to read in school but as high-quality literature. Students in US schools have a history of reading texts in the Eurocentric canon. Some of these texts will no doubt be included in your curriculum, so you and your students need to question together how various texts are selected for study and what values are attached to them. Together you also need to identify and describe the literary value of the diverse texts your students are reading.

Ways in which you can help your students understand and appreciate literature, as well as develop their critical literacy, are:

- Every six to nine weeks, list the texts students have read during that time.

- In a chart, categorize each text according to genre, time period (when the text was written, as well as when the story is set), cultures represented (the author's and in the work), language in which it was written (or languages represented in), and the basic storyline or content.

- Have students journal individually (and/or in partnered, small-group, and whole-class discussions) the parallels and distinctions they notice among these texts.

- Create partnerships or groups of students who have read texts representing different cultural and linguistic backgrounds, time periods, and genres (perhaps also include a canonical text the class has read together). Have students discuss what they notice about how authors use their life experiences, culture, and language as tools in crafting literary works.

- Invite students to share their thinking about the value, importance, or success of the various texts they have read and why they think the way they do.

These activities and conversations help students build their own definitions of what makes a high-quality text or reading experience. Students develop the capacity to read many kinds of texts and notice how authors draw from their cultural and linguistic knowledge, their knowledge of a particular issue or content, and literary strategies or processes to create compelling works. Students also build their critical literacy — their ability to identify and critique underlying ideologies about high- and low-status cultural and linguistic features that influence how school texts are selected (Lee 2007).

Assign Diverse Forms of Student Writing

The diverse texts students read become models for their own writing. The standardized writing curriculum dictates the genre, content, and language of students' writing. Students are usually responding to literature they have read, with you as their sole audience. Using a more adaptive and imaginative approach to writing instruction, you'll create a variety of writing opportunities for students that allow them to write for different purposes and audiences — academic, personal, social, and political — and explicitly draw on all of their cultural and linguistic knowledge and skills when composing. Vary your writing curriculum by introducing these writing and instructional approaches:

- Have students write in one or more journals, several times a week. They might keep an inquiry or research journal for long-term projects, a reading journal or notebook in connection with the texts they read, and a writer's notebook in which they learn to take on the habits and identity of a writer. Writing like this supports students' academic work and encourages them to think about and discuss that work with others. It also builds students' identity and practice as a reader and a writer, both in and outside school.

- Have students synthesize a long-term project (an inquiry project or other unit of study) in a lengthier piece of writing. Writing about a language inquiry project develops well-informed critical understanding about diversity and equity in school and social life. Memoir writing is an opportunity for students to draw on their culture, language, and life experience to produce a literary work that is personally, socially, and academically significant.

- Give students opportunities to write in various languages. Have them select language that best supports the thinking and writing they are trying to accomplish and that creates the emphasis and impact they wish the text to have.

- Provide diverse audiences for students' writing that are suited to the purpose of their texts. A reader's journal can be shared with classmates and people outside school with whom students talk about books. Students can share their inquiry projects with family, community members, school personnel, and others they want to influence with the results of their research.

Inquire into Student Writing

Students' writing should become the subject of investigation (Canagarajah 2006). Students should have many opportunities to develop, describe, and assess the goals, processes, and outcomes of the texts they compose. Standardization skewed toward analyzing texts written by others trumpets the message that their own writing is a poor imitation of "real" writing, not worthy of being read or thought about by others. When we don't spend time studying students' own writing, the message persists that the purpose of writing in school is purely functional — to fulfill the teacher's or the curriculum's expectations and earn a passing grade. Adaptive and imaginative instruction creates opportunities for students to learn about the many composition tools available (including their language practices and cultural experiences) and decide how to use these tools to achieve the varied purposes of the many kinds of texts they create.

In order to improve their understanding of the composition process, have students ask themselves the following questions as they are developing ideas, working on drafts, and discussing their final products:

- What are/were your goals or purposes for composing this text?

- Who is the intended audience(s)? Who else might come across this text, other than your intended audience(s)? What response do you hope to achieve?

- What resources or tools do you need/did you use to produce this text — both physical (such as mentor texts) and social or intellectual (personal experiences or cultural knowledge, knowledge acquired relative to the content or issue, suggestions of your peers and others, language practices)?

- In what ways is your text successful?

- How do you plan to share your work and hear from your intended audience, and what will you do with their feedback?

By paying this kind of attention to composition — to the content of the texts they produce and the processes they use to do so — students think through and make explicit the intentions behind the moves they are making — for themselves, you as their teacher, and their peers. They think about the particular linguistic (and other) tools and strategies they are employing to carry out their designs, and the effects they intend their language and literacy choices to have on their texts and their audiences. By regularly composing multicultural and multilingual texts and having academic conversations about their design and effect, your students will acquire a stronger understanding of how to apply their cultural and linguistic resources to their academic learning. Students will develop the full range of their cultural and linguistic repertoires and become more expert at using these resources productively.

References

Ball, Arnetha F., Allison Skerrett, and Ramon Antonio Martinez. 2010. *Research on Diverse Students in Culturally and Linguistically Complex Language Arts Classrooms.* In *Handbook of Research on Teaching the English Language Arts*, Third edition, eds. D. Lapp and D. Fisher, 22–28. New York: Routledge.

Bomer, Randy. 2011. *Building Adolescent Literacy in Today's English Classrooms.* Portsmouth, NH: Heinemann.

Canagarajah, A. Suresh. 2006. "The Place of World Englishes in Composition. Pluralization continued." *College Composition and Communication* 57 (4): 586–619.

Christenbury, Leila, Randy Bomer, and Peter Smagorinsky. 2009. *Handbook of Adolescent Literacy Research.* New York: Guilford Press.

Fu, Danling, and Jennifer M. Graff. 2009. "The Literacies of New Immigrant Youth." In *Handbook of Adolescent Literacy Research,* eds. L. Christenbury, R. Bomer, and P. Smagorinksy, 400–414. New York: Guilford Press.

García Sánchez, I., and M. F. Orellana. 2006. "The Construction of Moral and Social Identity in Immigrant Children's Narratives-in-Translation." *Linguistics and Education* 17: 209–239.

Hargreaves, Andy, and Allison Skerrett. 2012. "School Leadership for Diversity." In *Encyclopedia of Diversity in Education,* ed. J. A. Banks, 1886–1891.

Lee, Carol D. 2007. *Culture, Literacy, and Learning: Taking Bloom in the Midst of a Whirlwind.* New York: Teachers College Press.

Martínez, Ramon A. 2010. "Spanglish as Literacy Tool: Toward an Understanding of the Potential Role of Spanish-English Code-switching in the Development of Academic Literacy." *Research in the Teaching of English* 45 (2): 124–149.

Martínez-Roldán, Carmen, and Maria E. Fránquiz. 2009. "Latina/o Youth Literacies: Hidden Funds of Knowledge." In *Handbook of Adolescent Literacy Research,* eds. L. Christenbury, R. Bomer, and P. Smagorinksy, 323–342. New York: Guilford Press.

National Center for Educational Statistics. 2013. "Characteristics of Public and Private Elementary and Secondary Schools in the United States: Results from the 2011–12 Schools and Staffing Survey." Washington, DC: US Department of Education.

New London Group. 1996. "A Pedagogy of Multiliteracies: Designing Social Futures." *Harvard Educational Review* 66: 60–92.

Orellana, Marjorie F., and Jennifer F. Reynolds. 2008. "Cultural Modeling: Leveraging Bilingual Skills for School Paraphrasing Tasks." *Reading Research Quarterly* 43 (1): 48–65.

Owodally, Ambarin M. A. 2011. "Multilingual Language and Literacy Practices and Social Identities in Sunni Madrassahs in Mauritius: A Case Study." *Reading Research Quarterly* 46 (2): 134–155.

Paris, Django. 2011. *Language Across Difference: Ethnicity, Communication, and Youth Identities.* New York: Cambridge University Press.

Reynolds, Jennifer F., and Marjorie F. Orellana. 2009. "New Immigrant Youth Interpreting in White Public Space." *American Anthropologist* 111 (2): 211–223.

Skerrett, Allison. 2012. "Languages and Literacies in Translocation: Experiences and Perspectives of a Transnational Youth." *Journal of Literacy Research* 44 (4): 364–395.

———. 2013. "Building Multiliterate and Multilingual Writing Practices and Identities." *English Education* 45 (4): 322–360.

———. (Under Review). *Literacy Education Across Transnational Settings.* New York: Teachers College Press.

Skerrett, Allison, and Andy Hargreaves. 2008. "Student Diversity and Secondary School Change in a Context of Increasingly Standardized Reform." *American Educational Research Journal* 45 (4): 913–945.

Skerrett, Allison, and Randy Bomer. 2011. "Borderzones in Adolescents' Literacy Practices: Connecting Out-of-School Literacies to the Reading Curriculum." *Urban Education* 46 (6): 1256–1279.

———. 2013. "Recruiting Languages and Lifeworlds for Border-Crossing Compositions." *Research in the Teaching of English* 47 (3): 313–337.

Vygotsky, L. S. 1978. *Mind in Society.* Cambridge, MA: Harvard University Press.

Zúñiga, Victor, and Edmund T. Hamann. 2009. "Sojourners in Mexico with US School Experience: A New Taxonomy for Transnational Students." *Comparative Education Review* 53 (3): 329–353.

 **Allison Skerrett** *is an associate professor in the Department of Curriculum and Instruction at the University of Texas at Austin. She is a former secondary school English teacher of culturally and linguistically diverse students. Her current teaching and research foci are in the areas of adolescent literacy, secondary English curriculum and instruction, and sociocultural influences on teaching and learning. She can be reached at askerrett@utexas.edu.*

Love in a Time of Mapping

William Kist

As I write this chapter about imagining my ideal school, my worlds are colliding, juxtaposing the old and the new. While I'm in the process of going through some old files from my days as a high school teacher (to prepare to teach a certain methods course for the first time), I'm also looking forward in a completely new way. For the first time, when I imagine my ideal school, I'm imagining it for my own children. In June 2012, my wife, Stephanie, and I welcomed into the world our beautiful triplets — Mariel, Liam, and Vivienne. When I think about what I already know about teaching and learning, I now can't help but cast these ideas in light of dreaming big for Mariel, Liam, and Viv.

Stealing down into the basement after my children are asleep, I break open these old files, some of which have not been looked at in more than twenty years. Why did I keep them? As I look through them, I think — how could I not keep them? As I turn the pages, the voices of my former students come back to me in a rush; I hear them exactly as they were — entering the school each morning, shouting, laughing. It was the time of day, for me, when it was most exciting to be a high school teacher. I still remember the charge of anticipation I felt as the students poured through the doors.

What's hard to believe is that my teaching days were done in a mostly analog world. Even though so much has changed since then, it's amazing how much these documents bring back occurrences and happenings that seem quite current and relevant. What's obvious to me is what endures — coalescing through all these faded stories are filaments of love. What I'm coming to realize, as I've been drafting this chapter, is that the distinctive desired feature of my ideal school would be that all of the school's teachers would love all of the children there as they would their own.

Education at Its Core

I'm using the word *love* in terms of its meaning *in loco parentis* — the teacher as situated in place of the students' parents and loving those students as a parent would. But, still, I realize I'm risking some criticism by associating the word *love* with teaching and learning. Certainly viewing the teacher as parent has not always been the primary impetus in deciding what goes on in American classrooms, and my emphasis on love might be seen as not only overly sentimental, but also as misplaced, even inappropriate. Learning to read and write and all the "content" that goes with it is serious business! We know that the roots of literacy in ancient societies, for example, began mostly for functional, commercial uses (Harris 1989). For centuries, literacy education existed only for a small group of elites, and even in our relatively new democratic country, teaching young people to read and write quite often had goals that couldn't exactly be termed "altruistic." Whether the main objective was attempting to indoctrinate religious dogma in the 1600s, or trying to ignite secular nationalistic unity in the 1700s (Myers 1996), those in positions of power did not necessarily see "love" as a schools' main reason for being. Even thinking of people under the age of eighteen as "children" — a separate class of humanity — is a construct that is less than two hundred years old (Mintz 2004; Savage 2007). As late as the 1800s, a child's mind was seen simply as a muscle that could best be exercised by rote memorization and monotonous drill (Kliebard 2004). Even such a progressive promoter as Horace Mann would struggle with the question that had preoccupied theorists from Plato to Rousseau — "How does one free a child and shape him or her at the same time?" (Cremin 1964). But if each child could be viewed in a foremost way through a lens of love, wouldn't that render such a binary-based question if not moot, at the very least articulated too starkly?

As I work my way slowly through my old files, I find curriculum documents with sentences that now seem quaint, yet breathless in their firm certainty of correctness. It makes me wonder what will be thought of today's phrases twenty-five years from now. How will Common Core wording, such as "college- and career-ready" and "read like detectives," play out several decades from now? As I examine these old files of mine as a new father and see the rhetoric of those older times now faded, what seems obvious to me now is that I (and many of us at the time) may have missed the forest for the trees. As Nel Noddings put it: "When we put together a curriculum, there is an assumption that it will somehow meet students' needs. Often in our day-to-day work, we forget about the connection between curriculum and needs or suppose it has already been established in a long-standing body of goals and objectives" (Noddings 2005, p. 149). The irony is that now, more than at any other time in history, I believe it's possible to really know our students and lovingly teach them to an individual extent that was not possible even as recently as five years ago. How I wish I had some of what is available now for classrooms when I was teaching.

What Gets Lost

As I look back on my classroom teaching, I wish I had indeed done more to reach out to my students in that spirit of love. And my regret is fueled even more by the knowledge that I had so much more freedom than most of today's teachers do. The latitude I had, in retrospect, was breathtaking in comparison with today's prevalent rigid curriculum maps and scripted instruction. It makes me see, even more, my many missed chances. When I started teaching "back in the day," I remember only being handed a blank gradebook and a key to the school's storeroom. In that storeroom were many class sets of various paperback books, along with an approved list of about fifty different works I could teach per grade level. Which works I taught and which order I taught them in were choices that were completely up to me. On my own, I decided to start my ninth graders with *Lord of the Flies* (Golding 1954), and my students and I never looked back as we explored the symbolism of Golding's work, not to mention all the work's literary allusions and classic themes relevant to their own high school experiences. I believe I did carve out some space in Room 208 for learning experiences that allowed my students and I to really identify with one another and the texts we were reading. Perhaps unwittingly, I tried to create a space where we could read and write and look at all kinds of texts together, within a safe learning environment of love and respect. For one thing, I felt just as oppressed as my students were. I also admired them. I felt that they carried on, so many of them, with a joy of spirit and a sense of humor, in the midst of sometimes dreary, even horrific conditions. It wasn't until April that someone bothered to hand me the official district curriculum.

But I still have regrets. I feel that I loved my students and that we learned much together, but I still think I lost a lot of them. What often brought this home to me was seeing my former students after they had graduated. I was sometimes shocked by their appearances. I'm not speaking to the fact that they had grown into adulthood. Rather, what was most apparent was that it seemed that most, if not all, of the light had gone out of their eyes. There was no doubt that they had come back as "grown-ups," showing off their military uniforms or pictures of their families. I would wonder what had happened to all the laughter, all the questions. It seemed that, post-graduation, they became monochromatic versions of their former rainbow selves. "Oh, well," I would think, "life goes on, long after the thrill of living is gone," and I would go back to working with my current students. Life went on for me, too.

And there's the rub — I don't think we have done a good enough job of loving our kids into adulthood. While we put so much of an emphasis in our society on giving (many of) our kids their fair share of "Disney moments," we have neglected to think about the transition into their grown-up years, when we won't be around. "It's all about the kids," we say. But what we get with that approach is just another generation of kids who grow up to say, "It's all about the kids." Why couldn't the ability to socially network, to read and write in multimodal forms, to initiate new ways of "doing school," open up a vista of continuing to grow and learn for a lifetime? The intent would not be to prolong childhood or infantilize our young adults, but to start each student on a path that has more than a few moments of the kind of fervor and discovery that pervaded those early morning high school hallways.

What Remains

What's frustrating to me about not realizing this potential is that I truly believe we are closer than ever to being able to actualize truly differentiated classrooms for masses of students. But we're not taking advantage of these possibilities. Sadly, I believe that many fast-food restaurants do a better job of individualizing their interactions with customers than we educators do individualizing our interactions with students. The main focus of traditional school efforts since the 1980s has continued to be the yearly administering of standardized tests in which students read random decontextualized passages and then have to answer multiple-choice questions to make sure they are demonstrating "comprehension." We have so clearly been missing the opportunity to love each of our kids, and this is especially maddening now that we have so much more capacity to do so.

As I think about a school for Mariel, Liam, and Viv, I imagine one that provides space for developing passions and habits of work that will sustain "flow" states (Cziksentmihalyi 1990) beyond those prescribed years from birth to eighteen. Although I am not a technological determinist, I do believe that we now have the tools to individualize our classrooms in much deeper and meaningful ways, using new media and forms of storage. Instead of having the "flow" state reduced to a mere gurgle upon commencement, it's possible that the new ways we have of connecting will allow us to help our students to keep "the thrill of living" that, for too many of our graduates, seems not to "go on." As I witness the individual personalities develop in my own very young children, I see confirmed a long-held, if unrealized, key principle of mine and many other educators — that we must figure out a way to do a better job of meeting each child where he or she is.

In my first publication (Kist 2000), I wrote about this ideal of differentiation as I speculated about the ways new media could be used in classrooms. In such a differentiated school, I wrote:

> There would be many studios under one roof. There would be studios for writing; for shooting films and videos; for drawing, making sculpture, and shaping metals and other materials; for dancing; and for acting and directing. There would also be science and math studios (perhaps still called

"laboratories"). There would be studios for growing and studying living things. Each teacher would have studio space of his or her own, making his or her own meaningful work in multimedia, serving to model for students. The school would not only have multiple venues for expression, it would have multiple venues for 'receiving' expression: areas for reading; places to view works of art and theater, dance, and film; spaces for experiencing exhibits of science and math. The literacy teacher in such a school would become a coach of human expression." (Kist 2000, p. 712)

The vision I had is now realizable simply using the smartphones that many students carry around in their pockets. And yet it seems that few schools are taking advantage of the tools that are currently available that would make the kind of individualized instruction described above easier and more manageable than ever before. Today many apps exist that allow students to become curators of their own learning. Whether they capture their learning via free apps such as Mahara (https://mahara.org) or Three Ring (http://threering.com) and then exhibit their learning via Voicethread (http://voicethread.com) or Weebly (www.weebly.com), any student with access to a smartphone and the Internet can provide ample demonstration of learning. Never before has portfolio assessment been so easy and cheap to set up. Portfolio assessment is, of course, a means of assessing students holistically, allowing for teachers and students to set up learning goals that may be achieved in true multimodal, self-paced fashion. Each student could assemble many different "artifacts" that demonstrate their learning. A key element of portfolio assessment has also been student self-assessment — the student takes an active role in considering how much or how little he or she has grown and what their next steps should be. This kind of self-assessment has never been more doable. Students can demonstrate their "reading" and "writing" of a wide variety of kinds of texts, and how they annotated them, using apps such as Subtext (www.subtext.com), and how they processed them, using venues such as Slideshare (www.slideshare.net) or Dropbox (www.dropbox.com). There are also, of course, any number of platforms for managing such portfolios virtually, such as Edmodo (www.edmodo.com), Schoology (www.schoology.com), Collaborize (www.collaborizeclassroom.com),

Moodle (https://moodle.org), or simply creating a Google site, to name just a few. Even just setting up a blog or class wiki with individual student pages is something that can be done in a relatively short time and that allows students to demonstrate their research, their reading, and how they are making sense of what they are learning. In short, it has never been so possible for teachers to individualize learning and for students to represent their learning, thoughts, and emotions in so many ways. Another benefit of these online sharing systems is that the sharing doesn't have to end at graduation time.

There are definitely teachers who are making the most of the affordances of these new forms of representation. I meet them whenever I visit schools, and I meet them online. And yet they always seem somewhat isolated in their schools. People often ask me to point them to schools where new media are being used systemically across grade levels. Unfortunately, I don't have an answer for these queries. I can point to many individual teachers, but not entire schools, much less entire school districts. Of the six teachers I profiled in my first book, *New Literacies in Action* (Kist 2005), five of them have retired or changed jobs, and their work has not been carried on by remaining colleagues. For whatever reasons, these ideas don't usually seem to catch on beyond a core group of teachers in each school. And when I talk to parents of young children, the trend seems to be, in their experiences, elementary teachers who send home packets of hard-copy worksheets for the children to complete each week and turn back by Friday. These worksheets are then "graded" by the teacher using a red pen, and then the student gets another packet of worksheets to work on for the next week. I've also been in elementary classrooms where I've seen iPads being used as a one-room schoolteacher might have used slates. And so on and so on.

Actually, I shouldn't denigrate slates. And it's really not about the technology. My grandmother was a one-room schoolteacher in the early 1920s in rural Ohio, and she used to talk about having to prepare individualized lessons for seven grades of students. In her classroom, there were one or two students who were in each grade, from one through eight (except for grade seven, she would say). She used to have to write out completely different activities and lessons for each group of students to do. Some grades would have only one student who needed lessons for that grade. My grandmother spoke of being worn out — her own mother worried that she was working too hard. As a former teacher who lived into her nineties, however, my grandmother's hard work was rewarded by students who still kept in touch with her. My grandmother individualized her lessons and loved her students. In the end, it doesn't really matter if it's a slate or an iPad.

Epilogue

As I come to the close of my file excavation, my greatest worries are saved for those students who have not kept in touch, those students with whom I failed to connect even when they were in my classroom. These are the students who haunt most teachers, I think. We still love them, even if they don't love us. Even when they are with us, in class, they might be physically present, but they are otherwise vacant and therefore essentially absent. Perhaps if we strove to create the most loving of learning environments, we wouldn't have so many students who are "checked out." These are the students for whom we must be the most imaginative, creative, and, yes, loving. Anyone who has spent any time at all in a classroom, virtual or not, knows a few of these "remote" students. One of these students, for me, was named Akua.

During my last year of teaching I ended up chaperoning the prom. I often taught seniors and would find myself taking part in all of the rituals of those last days before summer. Prom is kind of a big deal even for teachers. At least it was for me. (It's a big deal for many parents, too, but that's another, not unrelated, story.) There was a huge turnout at this last prom I chaperoned. What made this event extra otherworldly for me was that it was taking place in the very same location as my own high school prom, which had occurred not that many years before. Indeed, it seemed that not much had changed about that setting during the intervening years. There was the same twilight; the same dim, hazy light seeping indoors; and the same balmy, early summer breeze blowing in through the tall, heavy, wooden-framed windows. As I was noticing this breeze, I was startled by someone tapping me on the shoulder.

It was one of my students, Akua, who had come up behind me. "May I have this dance?" she politely asked. Akua was a statuesque African American girl who that night wore a glamorous, flowing white dress. She looked nothing like the girl she usually appeared to be, hunched over in my second-period British Literature class, saying little.

I didn't normally dance with students, but Akua was insistent. I remember that she held onto my arm with a kind of determined grip that was very intent. I went ahead and agreed, but I stood woodenly, swaying on my two feet as we danced. I don't think she said much. I didn't say much either. I remember the other kids dancing by, saying, "Hey, Mr. Kist!" I smiled gamely. Throughout the song (Extreme's "More Than Words"), Akua seemed to have a kind of death grip on me. When the song was over, I started to go, but she didn't let go of me. I remember having the feeling that there was something not so ordinary or "fun" about this situation. Her hold on me was not playful. The music started up again, and we danced. I remember that I didn't try to make a joke or say much at all. The song ended and we parted.

A few days later, I noticed that Akua was not in class. I found out later that she had run away. With only a few days left before graduation, she was gone. Her anguished father called me and some of the other teachers to ask if we had any information about Akua, all to no avail. She never showed up at school again. No one knew what had happened to her. Her family was, obviously, very concerned. At the commencement ceremony, her name was not called.

When I was a classroom teacher, I felt that my students were heroes. I loved them, and, in many ways, I think I failed them. I'm really not fishing for compliments here. I just think I could have done a better job of loving them across that great divide between childhood and adulthood. I do know, with complete certainty, that at least I did love them. And maybe that was worth a lot. I often think of so many of them, and I really miss them. And, in fact, I imagine a school someday where Mariel, Liam, and Viv are loved by all their teachers, in a thoughtful, intentional way that sustains them well into adulthood. "I do know that I love you, and I know that if you love me too what a wonderful world this would be."

About seven or eight years after that prom, I was stunned to run into Akua. She seemed to recognize me immediately and I her; she looked remarkably the same. Her story came back to me in a rush, even though it had been nearly a decade. I concernedly asked how she was doing. She replied that she had ended up going to a prominent university and graduated with a bachelor's degree. "We were worried about you!" I said. She just looked at me and laughed, as if it were nothing.

References

Cremin, Lawrence. A. 1961. *The transformation of the school: Progressivism in American Education, 1876–1957*. New York: Vintage Books.

Csikszentmihalyi, Mihaly. 1990. *Flow: The Psychology of Optimal Experience*. New York: HarperCollins.

French, Thomas. 1996. *South of Heaven: Welcome to High School at the End of the 20th Century*. New York: Pocket.

Golding, William. 1954. *Lord of the Flies*. New York: Perigee.

Harris, William V. 1989. *Ancient Literacy*. Cambridge, MA: Harvard University Press.

Kist, William. 2005. *New Literacies in Action: Teaching and Learning in Multiple Media*. New York: Teachers College Press.

———. 2000. "Beginning to Create the New Literacy Classroom: What Does the New Literacy Look Like?" *Journal of Adolescent & Adult Literacy* 43: 710–718.

Kliebard, Herbert M. 2004. *The Struggle for the American Curriculum 1893–1958*, 3rd ed. New York: RoutledgeFalmer.

Mintz, Steven. 2004. *Huck's Raft: A History of American Childhood*. Cambridge, MA: The Belknap Press of Harvard University Press.

Noddings, Nel. 2005. "Identifying and Responding to Needs in Education." *Cambridge Journal of Education* 35 (2): 147–159.

Savage, Jon. 2007. *Teenage: The Creation of Youth Culture*. New York: Viking.

William Kist *is an associate professor at Kent State University, where he teaches literacy methods courses for preservice teachers in English education. Having presented nationally and internationally with three books and more than fifty articles and book chapters to his credit, Bill writes for* The Cleveland Plain Dealer *as a member of the National Book Critics Circle. He can be found online at: www.williamkist.com.*

Schools as Centers for Inquiry

Marilyn Cochran-Smith and Rebecca Stern

There is an unusual kind of freedom that comes with being invited to write about our vision of what schools might be without having to take into account the multiple obstacles that stand in the way. In today's accountability context, with its intense emphasis on monitoring, surveillance, and evaluation of teachers — often with the presumption that teachers are the root cause of educational failure in the first place — most alternative visions seem unlikely, if not impossible. Indeed none of us has escaped the impact of today's "common sense" notion of how to fix schools by aggressively weeding out the "bad teachers" who fail to boost students' test scores.

The media has hammered this message home, as a 2010 *Newsweek* story (Thomas and Wingert 2010) illustrates. The magazine cover featured a traditional schoolroom blackboard with the sentence, "We must fire bad teachers," chalked over and over again down the board. Halfway down, in striking yellow letters, was the caption, "THE KEY TO SAVING AMERICAN EDUCATION." The backdrop for the *Newsweek* story was the changing politics of education, but the most powerful images in the story were of "bad teachers" — including teachers charged with incompetence, misconduct, and even criminal acts — and the unsubtle implication that the problem of "bad teachers" is not isolated but, in fact, widespread.

Embedded in the *Newsweek* story were three positive examples of teachers. Teachers in inner-city KIPP (Knowledge Is Power Program) schools were described as being so dedicated that they give students their cell phone numbers so they can always reach them. The authors commented, however, that the high attrition rate of KIPP teachers was perhaps because "teaching in an inner-city school is a little like going into the Special Forces in the military, a calling for only the chosen few" (26). The second positive example was contained in a quote from former Washington, DC, superintendent of schools, Michelle Rhee, who said, "When I visit schools, sometimes I see pure magic. People in unbelievably crappy school buildings, dealing with terrible conditions, whose classrooms are alive with learning. They are just unbelievable" (32). The third example was from one of the author's own Catholic school experiences in the 1960s, when the nuns easily kept very large classes in line — with hands folded, eyes front, and mouths shut — while unruly children were sent to the corner or "beaned" with an eraser by at least one nun with an "amazing pitching arm" (33).

Teachers as Inquirers, Schools as Inquiry Centers

Our vision of "good teachers" and "good schools" is dramatically different from these dubious images of good teachers as combat troops, magicians, and baseball pitchers. In contrast, we envision teachers (and students) who work from an ongoing inquiry stance on teaching, learning and teaching in schools that are organized to foster a culture of inquiry. This is not a new idea. Almost fifty years ago, Robert Schaefer (1967) published a little-known book titled *The School as a Center of Inquiry*. In schools that center on inquiry, teachers, administrators, and students learn by asking meaningful questions about curriculum, subject matter, skills, and the world itself. Based on the premise that teachers are professionals who should be engaged in, excited by, and reflective about their work, Schaefer speculated that "observing adults honestly wrestling with intellectual problems might win more youngsters to the life of the mind than any other experience the school could devise" (77).

Schaefer's ideas are consistent with the notion of "inquiry as stance," conceptualized by Marilyn Cochran-Smith, the first author of this chapter, and Susan Lytle

(Cochran-Smith and Lytle 1999, 2009). As Cochran-Smith and Lytle suggest, to call inquiry a "stance" is to regard inquiry as a worldview, a critical habit of mind, and a dynamic way of knowing in the world of educational practice that carries across professional careers and educational settings. This is different from inquiry understood as a time- and place-bounded classroom research project, as a method, or as a set of steps for solving problems. When inquiry is a project, the message is that inquiry is something turned off and on at given points in time. When inquiry is a method for solving problems, it positions practitioners as receivers of information, with little space for questioning the ways problems are posed in the first place or for problematizing the terms and logic of larger frames. Fundamental to inquiry as a stance is the idea that educational practice is not simply instrumental in the sense of figuring out how to get things done, but also (and more importantly), "it is social and political in the sense of deliberating about what gets done, why to get it done, who decides, and whose interests are served" (Cochran-Smith and Lytle 2009, p. 121). Cochran-Smith and Lytle link inquiry to democratic purposes and social justice ends. They emphasize that in schools organized to support inquiry, communities are not simply tools for making teachers more efficient. Rather, communities are the mechanism through which teachers and other practitioners come together over time to reflect deeply and question what they are doing. This includes rethinking taken-for-granted practices and activities, raising questions about new initiatives and reforms that are often imposed on schools from external authorities, and supporting one another's efforts to construct democratic curriculum and pedagogy. First and foremost, inquiry communities acknowledge that teaching is complex and uncertain work that requires collaborative problem posing and joint consideration of multiple meanings and possibilities, rather than work that is driven by the singular pursuit of "right answers."

In the remainder of this chapter, we expand our vision of schools as places where teachers are regarded as professionals, where teachers and students are inquirers, and where the culture is organized to sustain and support ongoing questioning and reflection. We elaborate this vision using examples from three different schools.

Inquiry-based Curriculum and Pedagogy

In schools organized to sustain teachers' and students' ongoing reflection and questioning, both curriculum and pedagogy are inquiry-based, which also engenders inquiry learning on the part of students. Teachers who see themselves as knowers, ask questions and pose problems, and so do their students. Schools organized as centers for inquiry encourage joint problem posing among faculty and foster the development of rigorous, engaging, and student-centered curriculum through teacher-inquiry communities. Although one goal of inquiry-centered schools is that all students have basic knowledge and skills, it is as important that students learn to raise questions about the sources and uses of knowledge and that they develop the skills of critique, deliberation, and analysis.

King Middle School in Portland, Maine, serves here as an illustration of inquiry-based curriculum and pedagogy. King is a well-known expeditionary learning school where Rebecca Stern, the second author of this chapter, is working as an administrative intern. At King, teachers meet together in teams for one week every summer and for eighty minutes every other day during the school year to plan and reflect upon the "expeditions," or interdisciplinary units, that are the foundation of the school's curriculum. King eighth-grade teacher, Peter Hill, recently told us that teachers plan their expeditions by asking, "What do we need to be teaching? How can we do it in an authentic, innovative way?" Teachers choose a compelling topic that aligns with the learning standards for each course and that engages students. Working together, teachers then create expeditions that are standards-based, authentic, and exciting. Expeditions are wide-ranging in topic and connected to current events in which students have expressed interest, such as invasive species in Maine's oceans, the life experiences of refugees who have resettled in Portland, and local political issues such as the building of an oil pipeline off the coast. Students learn to gather and critique information from a variety of sources about these topics, always questioning the purpose, perspective, and legitimacy of the sources. They then demonstrate their learning through an authentic public event or product that shows their own particular understanding of the topic.

For example, Peter Hill described the process he and his eighth-grade team used to create an expedition titled "reVOLT" about energy and energy transformation, topics that are central to the eighth-grade science standards. The eighth-grade team, which includes the science, social studies, English, and math teachers, asked, "How can we make [this topic] engaging to kids? How can we embed science for a purpose in the expedition?" In the reVOLT expedition, after doing a geological review of the state's land, students designed wind turbines using computer animation software. Then they completed actual applications for wind turbine sites and wrote letters to the town councils in the municipalities where they proposed the wind turbines be located (see Figure 1).

When curriculum and pedagogy are inquiry-based, they do not end when a particular unit ends. Rather, ongoing reflection on student learning and the curriculum itself are continuing parts of the process. At King, teachers engage in a formalized debriefing process to analyze the efficacy of the various parts of each unit. After the reVOLT unit, Hill reflected that the power of the curriculum lies in "personal authentic connection — kids designing real-world tools for someone in some place sparks an incredible amount of engagement and ingenuity." Through a rich, teacher-created curriculum planning process that connects curriculum and pedagogy to student-centered, authentic learning experiences, King Middle School fosters a culture of inquiry animated by excitement, curiosity, and meaningful learning for both teachers and students.

Structures That Foster Student Agency and Voice

As we showed in the example above, in schools organized as centers for inquiry, teachers work to build a curriculum that incorporates current events from local communities and that also draws on students' interests and experiences, which are regarded as resources and central drivers of student learning. As importantly, in schools that are centers for inquiry, teachers and other educators deliberately work to develop social, organizational, and intellectual structures that foster students' agency and voice. These structures reinforce and strengthen the capabilities of students, honoring their need to be in control of their own learning.

By way of illustration, we describe one aspect of Rebecca Stern's former classroom at a middle school in the low-income community of Dorchester, Massachusetts. Over several years, Stern noticed that middle school students in general, and

Figure 1: Excerpt from the reVOLT Expedition Planner

Excerpt: reVOLT Expedition Planner
King Middle School

COMPELLING/ENGAGING TOPIC:
Reinventing Visions of Life-Sustaining Technology

GUIDING QUESTION:
How can you transform energy to improve people's daily lives?

SAMPLE STANDARDS, LEARNING TARGETS, and ASSESSMENTS:
(Note: Each subject covered between three and five standards;
these are just a sample)

	Standard	Learning Target	Assessment
Science	Communicate, critique, and analyze their own scientific work and the work of other students Describe how science and technology can help address societal changes including population, natural hazards, sustainability, personal health and safety, and environmental quality	I can write a scientific lab report that has gone through the peer-review process. I can explain how humans' energy consumption impacts our Earth and society.	Lab report of wind turbine experiment KEDtalk PowerPoint (KED = King Engineering and Development)
English	Write arguments to support claims with clear reasons and relevant sources	I can support a claim with clear reasons and relevant evidence.	Persuasive letters to town councils

Math	Construct and interpret scatter plots for bivariate measurement data to investigate patterns of association between two quantities

Describe patterns such as clustering, outliers, positive or negative association, linear association, and nonlinear association | I can construct and interpret scatter plots and use a line of best fit, when appropriate. | Wind turbine data collection activity |
| **Social Studies** | Determine the central ideas or information of a primary or secondary source and analyze how they are developed over the course of the text | I can objectively summarize primary and secondary sources. | Turbine site plan |
| **Technology** | What is the process for developing potential design solutions? | I can design and build a model wind turbine that generates electricity. | Model wind turbine |

her own students in particular, were highly motivated by the quest for what they considered "justice" (or the elimination of "injustice"). The students wanted to be heard and understood—not only by adults, but also by each other—regarding issues ranging from ways to make sure everyone did his or her fair share of work in a group to consideration of whether or not the school's dress code was oppressive because it took away "personal style." Through weekly journal writing in her classroom, Stern noticed that her students remained calm and were engaged in learning when "justice" issues were addressed in ways the students found meaningful and when they felt their voices and concerns had been heard. In response, Stern initiated weekly classroom meetings during which students discussed the social, emotional, and political issues that had arisen over the course of the week. Initially run by

Stern, the meetings were eventually entirely student-led, which was no small task for a group of twenty-six fourteen-year-olds. Students proposed topics, interrogated each other's thinking, and posed questions that demanded honesty and self-reflection. Being empowered to address difficult issues had a spill-over effect on students' writing, group work, and interpersonal interactions as students developed the capacity to become leaders with both rights and responsibilities who could speak their minds and affect change.

While Stern's classroom meetings are an example of teacher inquiry leading to student inquiry and empowerment — practices that are central to our vision of schools as centers of inquiry — this example also illustrates the fundamentally different assumptions about students held by proponents of schools as centers of inquiry and those sometimes espoused by educators in low-income schools. For example, Goodman (2013) found that in schools she observed that were run by charter management organizations, low-income students of color experienced "a highly rule-ordered and regulated environment … [where] rules [were] enforced through continuous streams of reinforcements and penalties … [including] pervasive adult monitoring of students, targeting behaviors tangential to learning, attributing independent agency to children who deviated, and student derogation by adults" (89). In schools centered on inquiry, students are assumed to be curious and full of valued, rich knowledge, whereas in the schools Goodman (2013) described, students were assumed to be out of control and therefore dependent on adults to create strict boundaries. These stark differences in assumptions underscore the importance of a vision of schools as places where students can explore, create, imagine, and be respected. Instead, in some of today's schools, the coercive atmosphere may seem more akin to that of prisons than to centers of learning.

Democratic Leadership

A third aspect of schools organized as centers for inquiry is shared democratic leadership. Shared leadership stands in stark contrast to the *Newsweek*-type images — school administrators who are pitted against the teachers they lead and teachers who require constant monitoring to ensure adequate classroom performance. Our vision of schools as centers of inquiry where education professionals work with students is different in multiple ways from schools where leaders and teachers are assumed to be at odds with each other and where it is assumed that tight external accountability is the only way to shape schools up and force them to function productively.

Democratic leadership is also necessary if schools are to transcend the current focus of schooling on preparing students primarily for economic competition, instead supporting more democratic and social justice ends. Political philosopher Amy Gutmann (1987) suggests that education must be democratic in order to prepare students to participate thoughtfully in a democratic society. Democratic education rests on shared decision making by key stakeholders, including teachers. By creating school environments where teachers, administrators, students, and families all work together to provide and critique examples of what Gutmann (1987) calls "the good life," students develop the capacity to think critically about their own and others' lives, and how they might work to better them.

Here we use as an example the work of Gary McPhail, currently the head of the Meadowbrook Lower School, an independent elementary school in Weston, Massachusetts. Prior to becoming an administrator, McPhail taught first grade at Shady Hill School in Cambridge, Massachusetts, where he noticed that the personal narrative focus of the first-grade writing curriculum was particularly appealing to girls but not so appealing to many boys in his classes (McPhail 2009a, 2009b). By altering the curriculum and engaging in practitioner inquiry, McPhail found not only that boys and girls had differing literary interests, but also that both boys and girls performed at higher levels when they wrote in genres that were of interest to them. Based on these insights, McPhail invited other teachers to join him in an inquiry group focused on students' writing. Drawing on samples of children's writing from across the grades, the inquiry group worked together over several years to interrogate their writing practices, unpack their assumptions about boys and girls, and eventually create a new school-wide writing curriculum that responded to the interests of all writers. The new curriculum involved teaching multiple genres of writing, with new units deliberately designed to appeal to the interests of both boys and girls; this meant the writing curriculum shifted from a primary focus on personal narratives to a more inclusive approach that included letter writing, comic book creation, poetry, and science fiction, as well as personal narratives.

Gary was hired as the head of Meadowbrook Lower School in part because of his experience engaging in teacher research. Under his leadership, Meadowbrook teachers are now fully engaged in inquiry around issues of gender and learning. In an interview, McPhail commented to us that he "brought only the model [of inquiry], not the content" to Meadowbrook, emphasizing that faculty members themselves determined what they wanted to research. There are currently four faculty inquiry groups operating at Meadowbrook, which focus on gender and how boys and girls experience school differently. Each group formulates its own research questions and plans for design and implementation. Teachers volunteer to lead the groups and represent the full range of experience and diversity of Meadowbrook teachers. McPhail considers it his task as an administrator to help develop leaders within the groups and to capitalize on the experiences and values of the teachers themselves.

Because of his commitment to teachers' and students' experiences, voices, and knowledge, McPhail is a prime example of an administrator who values shared leadership, democratic participation, and authentic, intrinsic accountability. This example illustrates one vision of school leadership aimed at fostering a school-wide culture of inquiry in a democratically run school.

Schools as Centers for Inquiry: Concluding Comments

The illustrations in this chapter offer images of teachers and other educators that differ dramatically from the images of the "good" teachers in the *Newsweek* article with which this chapter began. The educators in our three examples work from an inquiry stance in schools that are exciting, authentic, respectful to their students, and inquiry-centered. Our examples reveal a reciprocal relationship. Schools organized as centers for inquiry have school-wide norms that shape the day-to-work of teachers, school leaders, and students. At the same time, teachers and students engaged in ongoing and collective question posing (and answering) shape and sustain cultures of inquiry. Right now there are many individual classrooms and whole schools scattered throughout the nation where inquiry is central and almost taken for granted as a way to think about new issues and to make decisions about teaching and learning. However, these exist as local pockets of inquiry-based schooling. Our vision for the future of public education is that these local pockets of inquiry-centered schooling grow and expand and that these examples become more widely known and understood as viable, exciting alternatives to an education that's centered on standardization, accountability, and testing. Inquiry-centered schools involve engaged teachers, students, and communities. Being empowered to question "business as usual" invites teachers and students to envision their own ideal learning environments, where all students have rich learning opportunities and resources and where all participants are respected and deeply engaged in learning.

References

Cochran-Smith, Marilyn, and Susan Lytle. 2009. *Inquiry as Stance: Practitioner Research for the Next Generation*. New York, NY: Teachers College Press.

———. 1999. "Relationship of Knowledge and Practice: Teacher Learning in Communities." In *Review of Research in Education* 24: 249–306. A. Iran-Nejad and C. Pearson, eds. Washington, DC: American Educational Research Association.

Gutmann, Amy. 1987. *Democratic Education.* Princeton, NJ: Princeton University Press.

McPhail, Gary. 2009a. "Teaching the 'Bad Boy' to Write." *Learning Landscapes* 3 (1): 89–104.

———. 2009b. "The 'Bad Boy' and the Writing Curriculum." In *Inquiry as Stance: Practitioner Research for the Next Generation*, ed. M. Cochran-Smith and S. Lytle, 93–212. New York: Teachers College Press.

Thomas, Evan, and Pat Wingert. 2010. "Why We Must Fire Bad Teachers." *Newsweek*, March 5, 2010.

 **Marilyn Cochran-Smith** *is Cawthorne Professor of Teacher Education and director of the Doctoral Program in Curriculum and Instruction at Boston College's Lynch School of Education. Dr. Cochran-Smith is a member of the National Academy of Education and a former president of the American Educational Research Association. She has published nine books and more than 175 articles, chapters, and editorials on practitioner inquiry, social justice, and teacher education.*

 **Rebecca Stern** *is a doctoral candidate in Curriculum and Instruction at Boston College, where she is studying the role of inquiry in teacher education and school leadership. She is a National Board Certified Teacher and has taught middle and high school social studies and English in Oakland, California; Dorchester, Massachusetts; and most recently, in Portland, Maine. Rebecca has been deeply involved in school reform efforts to increase equity for students, both as a classroom teacher and a school reform consultant.*

Are Classroom Practices Teaching Students to Be Independent Thinkers?

Historical Models for Literacy as a Tool of Agency

Gholnecsar E. Muhammad

When we say we want our students to become independent thinkers, do we mean *now* or are we hoping they gain their independence at some point in the future, *after* their time in our classrooms? Too often classrooms are saturated with instructional practices that do not advance students' ability to think independently. If we are not urgent in moving students forward intellectually, in powerful ways, we run the risk of merely hoping that they gain such proficiencies later in life. Classrooms in which literacy is viewed as a tool of intellectual development and independence are places of urgency, where reading and writing are neither deferred actions nor acts of mediocrity.

To grasp the weight of terms like *intellectual development* and *independence*, to keep them from becoming decontextualized jargon, let's look at a time when reading and writing were tools for advancing thinking and agency. Consider this statement from a public address by a member of an 1854 African American literary society:

There can be no more effective manner of elevating our people than by a spread of literature, and no more speedy way of demonstrating to those in authority in our government that we are susceptible of the highest degree of mental culture and worthy of the rights which have been so long withheld from us. (Martin 2002)

Does the speaker give literature and the role of literacy more power than we do in our classrooms? Throughout the 1800s, African American males in the United States created and sustained their own organizations for learning. African American people had limited to no rights within various social, political, and educational institutions in the United States, and consequently they relied on themselves to create and sustain their own organizations for learning. They also understood the power and need for community as a tool for identity. They consequently created their own agendas and claimed authority by organizing literary societies with a keen focus on nurturing their intellectual and literacy development. Consider the need for students in today's classrooms to create their own agendas or pathways, to claim their own authority over language, to proclaim to be readers, writers, and thinkers.

African American male literary societies emerged in 1828 with the installment of the Reading Room Society led by William Whipper (Porter 1936). Members of these societies met regularly to read, write, and discuss texts from all over the world. While their immediate aim was to improve and advance their literacy skills, their wider goal was to use the tools of reading, writing, and speaking to improve societal conditions for themselves and others (McHenry 2002). Society meetings were a refuge through which they came to know themselves and others, protect their cultural identity and their humanity (Tatum and Muhammad 2012), and acquire agency — the capacity, independence, and authority to assert their own voice, ideals, perspectives, and truths (Muhammad 2012b; Tatum 2013). They developed agency not just to push against but to create a "strategic making and remaking of selves, identities, activities, relationships, cultural tools, resources, and histories as they are embedded within relations of power" (Moje and Lewis 2007, p. 18).

As they sought to create and recreate their histories, identities, and literacies, they created literary outlets to sustain their efforts. The first newspaper owned and run by African Americans was *Freedom's Journal*, which began publication in 1827. The editors, who were literary society members, proclaimed their message of agency in the inaugural issue: "We wish to plead our own cause. Too long have others spoken for us." They were developing their own platform to express their narratives. Rather than allowing others to speak on their behalf, they created their own pathways to exert their truths. In much the same way, many classroom practices today do not allow students to infuse their identities and voices into curriculum and instruction. Instead, others have depicted the best ways for them to read, write, speak, and think. If instead we teach students how to use and make sense of language to assert their own voices, ideals, and perspectives, they will be able to use language confidently to understand the power and construction of knowledge. It is important for young people to experience agency so that they can own the development of their knowledge, reclaim the authority language gives them to know themselves, and feel confident engaging in acts of literacy.

The thread of human nature binds us to the past. We need to look at history not as fixed and separate from our present, but as a guide for our current practices. The texts that African American males read, wrote, and discussed in their literary societies allowed them to appropriate and own literacy endeavor. In terms of the literacy development of students in classrooms today, the question becomes: How can teachers lead students toward agency though literacy instruction? Particularly, how can reading and writing text be the vehicle for young people to own language and the authority it conveys? Although classrooms do not exactly mirror literary societies, several lessons gleaned from African American male literary societies have the potential to help teachers understand literacy and agency in the classroom.

- **Create spaces for students to analyze the stances and perspectives in texts.** To develop students' capacity to gain new knowledge, teachers should help them analyze and critique the stances and perspectives authors take in texts. For example, students should be invited to question the messages found in different types of texts — to think critically. Increasing such skills enables students to make sense of the world around them. Analyzing perspectives in texts was a key exercise undertaken by literary societies. A society member identified only as "A Young Man" wrote in *Freedom's Journal*:

> I do not expect a Debating Society will make us all Sheridans, but it will enlarge our powers of reasoning by teaching us to express our thoughts as brief as possible, and to the best advantage. It will also enable us to detect at a glance whatever sophistry is contained in the arguments of an opponent.

Students need to understand that texts, institutions, identity, are all authored; that anything created by human beings reflects the imprint of its creator(s); and that they can write to challenge these perspectives in a variety of ways. Do our students read texts not just for the author's intended message, but also for their own interpretations?

- **Create spaces for students to read texts that are responsive to their lives and times.** Rather than use the same reading lists year after year, teachers need to uncover the histories, identities, and literacies of the learners in their classroom and select texts that respond to these cultural strands. Students may then begin to draw more connections to their lives and the lives of others. This goes beyond reading texts relevant to students' ethnicity or gender. Students' identities are fluid and changing, and the texts they read must respond to their lives. Text selection and the development of libraries were central literary society endeavors. William Whipper advocated for "useful books [that will help us] form habits of close and accurate thinking [and] acquire a facility of classifying and arranging, analyzing, and comparing our ideas on different subjects." Texts are the core of all literacy endeavors. Are there a wide variety of texts in our classroom libraries that reflect the history, identity, and literacy of our students and that allow them to draw more connections to their lives and the lives of others?

- **Create spaces for students to write text openly and without apology.**
Alfred Tatum (2013) refers to such writing as "raw writing." Raw writing
helps students convey their own voices, ideals, and perspectives. Their
voices are honored — they begin to have confidence in their ability to
read and write, to seek literacy as a refuge and protection for their cultural identity. Writing without apology means having the freedom to express yourself (Muhammad 2012a) rather than respond to fixed writing
prompts that leave little or no opportunity to write openly with your
own voice, or that push you to write what you believe will please the
teacher (Muhammad 2012a). The preambles of African American male
literary societies are prime examples of unapologetic writing. Here's one
composed by the Adelphic Union in 1836 for the Promotion of Literature and Science:

  > We, the undersigned, impressed with the high importance of mental
  > improvement and progressive usefulness in obtaining a knowledge
  > of moral science and literature, and believing that an active interest
  > in these subjects among our community would be highly conducive
  > to this object, have associated ourselves together for the promotion
  > of the same. (Porter 1936)

  It conveys a clear agency to use language openly to project their message
  of pursuing self-advancement and social justice through literacy. How
  much self-directed reading and writing are the students in our classrooms
  doing right now?

- **Create a collective community of idiosyncratic readers and writers.**
In creating literary societies and publications, African American males
developed a self-renewing circle of writers and readers. The audience of
African American readers validated and invited African American writers. We build our identity through social groups. Do our students discuss what they read with their peers, consider what actions they'll take

based on what they read, and publish for authentic purposes? Are our classrooms cultivating a community of independent readers, writers, and thinkers?

The social and historical foundations of African Americans' literacy development are models for *all* students. They can be used to evaluate whether literacy is being offered as a tool for independence in any — and every — classroom. If students understand how literacy can be a tool to liberate themselves, they can use it as a tool to advance the lives of others. If we want to invite them into that self-renewing process, we need to demonstrate our belief in what literacy can be — by giving students the time and space to explore what literacy can do for them *right now*. The lessons briefly discussed above are a gauge we can use to consider the role of literacy and agency in our classrooms. If we strive to help our students become agentic learners, they will have the potential and susceptibility to use literacy as a tool to incite new thought and assert their own agency.

References

Lewis, Cynthia, Patricia Enciso, and Elizabeth B. Moje. 2007. *Reframing Sociocultural Research on Literacy: Identity, Agency, and Power.* Mahwah: Lawrence Erlbaum.

Martin, Tony. 2002. "The Banneker Literary Institute of Philadelphia: African American Intellectual Activism Before the War of the Slaveholders' Rebellion." *The Journal of African American History* 87: 303–22.

McHenry, Elizabeth. 2002. *Forgotten Readers: Recovering the Lost History of African American Literary Societies.* Durham: Duke University Press.

Muhammad, Gholnecsar E. 2012a. "Creating Spaces for Black Adolescent Girls to 'Write It Out!'" *Journal of Adolescent & Adult Literacy* 56 (3): 203–11.

———. 2012b. "The Literacy Development and Practices Within 1800s African American Literary Societies. *Black History Bulletin* 75 (1): 6–13.

Porter, Dorothy. 1936. "The Organized Educational Activities of Negro Literary Societies, 1828–1856." *Journal of Negro History* 5: 555–76.

Tatum, Alfred W. 2013. *Fearless Voices: Engaging a New Generation of African American Adolescent Male Writers.* New York: Scholastic.

Tatum, Alfred W., and Gholnecsar E. Muhammad. 2012. "African American Males and Literacy Development in Contexts That Are Characteristically Urban." *Urban Education* 47 (2): 434–63.

Gholnecsar E. Muhammad *is an assistant professor at Georgia State University teaching in the Department of Middle and Secondary Education. Her research interests are shaped around social and historical foundations of literacy development, writing pedagogy, and adolescent literacy.*

When Student Writers Ask, "Am I Allowed to . . . ?" the Answer Should Be "Yes!"

Olugbemisola Rhuday-Perkovich

The act of reading is not just decoding words on the page, it is a way into new worlds and it's a way to self-empower by seeing new versions of oneself and one's possibilities in the world. The act of writing stories, of telling one's own stories, is not just about expression, it is about transformation.

— LitWorld, Stand Up for Girls

"Why do you write?"

The question stopped me cold. I coughed, cleared my throat a few times. I had to resist the urge to revert to my adolescent shrug-and-mumble-incoherently staple. I wasn't sure what my answer was.

So I started writing to figure it out.

As a student writer, I saw writing as an opportunity to tell my story, no matter the assignment. For the outwardly well-behaved child I was, writing was release, freedom, and rebellion. It was, as bell hooks writes, "talking back."

Today, I'm the parent of a young writer. I'm also a children's author and educator, and I've had countless opportunities to engage with all kinds of learners in a variety of settings. I believe that all of them are writers, and I tell them so. Most of them have disagreed. On author visits, when I work through a writing prompt or exercise with students, the most common questions they ask begin with "Am I allowed to . . . ." And when I answer, "Of course! This is your story, your work, you're allowed to do anything, you won't get a grade, this is just for YOU," they regard me with surprise at best, distrust at worst. Our children are learning that they have no agency; that their ideas, their wonderings, and their worlds matter far less than their "results." How can we expect them to change the world? (Davis 2013).

The very act of writing, points out William Zinsser in *Writing To Learn*, "enables us to find out what we know — and what we don't know — about whatever we're trying to learn." In cognitive science, writing is described as an "ill-defined problem . . . for which there is no ready-made, best initial representation and no standard solution" (Bruer 1993). We speak often of the importance of developing students' critical thinking skills. If we are truly concerned with preparing our children for the "real world," why not fully enrich and transform teaching and learning of "the one school task that approximates the cognitive and creative demands of common real-world problems?" (Bruer 1993).

When we frame our writing instruction primarily in terms of checklists, structure, rubrics, five paragraphs with clear topic sentences and neat conclusions, we lose some of the most valuable and transferrable reasons to write — to think, to think about our thinking, and to work out how these thoughts will manifest themselves in our lives. Authentic, meaningful writing instruction can be used to process and reflect on our opinions, ideas, community, and society. To empower, to question, and to transform.

I was a quiet kid. In my home and the schools I went to there were clear lines of authority. I found freedom and discovered my creative and intellectual strengths through literacy. Our bookshelves were always packed full, overflow towers of books perched at their edges. The public library was my second home, and my mother provided me with a liberal supply of blank books, legal pads, and writing tools. I grew up doodling and scribbling, jotting down scraps of dialogue and description, even the occasional line from a favorite read. My father was very interested in fountain pens; we'd spend (what felt like) hours at the stationery store while he'd examine one that had been brought out from a glass case and lay nestled on a velvet bed. He'd try the ink and the flow, test-driving one after another on creamy sheets of paper.

I was fascinated.

No, I wasn't. I wasn't *that* much of a nerd.

Close, though.

The thing is, those moments happened, they were a regular part of my life. Because I was surrounded by people who took enormous pleasure in a literate life, I had the privilege of bring immersed in a literacy-rich environment that invited me into the wide-open expanse of possibility. I then comfortably transferred my concept of "my right to read and write freely" to my school life. Yes, I understood the rules and conventions and what would get me an "A," but I wrote at school for the same reason that I wrote at home — to find the joy, to make meaning, to discover, to figure things out, to explore, and to learn.

Student writers should be *allowed* to explore, to explain, to wonder, to wrestle. Writing instruction can be an authentic invitation to "say what you mean and mean what you say," to own one's work in myriad ways. Perhaps an emphasis on writing for empowerment will encourage students to trust their voices and tell their stories, to write for analysis, agency, and empathy. To stretch their imaginations into the beyond (Wang 2009). I believe that by transforming writing instruction, we can nurture learners who ask questions — learners who *never stop learning.* If we want to nurture thinkers, makers, collaborators, and leaders, let's write.

> *The purpose of education, finally, is to create in a person the ability to look at the world for himself, to make his own decisions.*
>
> — James Baldwin

As our students are increasingly exposed to — and sometimes assaulted by — the complexities of our world, we need to "help students use words as a passage into interrogating society. We need to move beyond sharing and describing our pain to examining why we're in pain" (Christensen 2000), perhaps imagining ways out. By giving students choice and providing opportunities to explore the meaning and context of their choices, we allow them to examine their ideas about the world they live in, and how they move about in the space they occupy. When we let students know that they are allowed to "trouble the waters" in writing, we are in effect telling them — and reminding ourselves — that their ideas matter. That — regardless of grades, scores, rank, status, race, gender, ethnicity — they have a story worth telling and sharing, and perhaps a responsibility, a need, to figure out what they'll do with it.

Why don't we give public school students, at all levels, real rooms of their own, daily writing time that engages any and every subject area? Time to play with words (Singer et al. 2006), language, and ideas, such as reflections on the science experiment that failed, or the best friend who is now a worst enemy. Harry Potter fan fiction or an original screenplay. A comic strip, graphic novel, or poem. With truly "free" writing opportunities, maybe taking three minutes from each class period for true "choice" writing, students can play with language through poetry, exercise their imaginations through writing science fiction or fantasy, or work up the nerve to settle a recess controversy by writing contemporary fiction.

Let us encourage conversations about writing — not only about craft, purpose, adding details, or raising the stakes — let's discuss the ideas, opinions, and inspirations that ground each piece of work. Writing from the heart in any genre takes courage, and given the room to wrestle and write, students can become increasingly equipped to hold themselves accountable for a large portion of their own learning. Many (but by no means all) of our children have access to powerful technology, but language — our ability to communicate and interpret effectively — remains among the most powerful tools of all. Today, we read and respond to a variety of media, engaging in almost continuous dialogue in digital spaces. As developing research demonstrates, there are exciting possibilities in the inclusion of social and emotional learning as an integral component of school curricula (Vega 2012) and practices (Jones et al. 2011), and writing that links both the personal and the public promotes empathy and connection. The "persuasive essays" that my father sometimes required as applications to attend a party or other sweaty evening event that involved lip gloss, were penned with feverish determination and focus. They meant something to me. And that process of writing, in retrospect, facilitated a communication between my father and me that we would not have otherwise had. Plus, I got to go to the parties. I went on to frame my college activism in my writing, in speeches, letters to the editor, local newspaper articles, appeals to administrators, and more. And I still went to the parties.

When people ask me for writing advice or tips, the first thing I say is: read. I believe that writing is nourished by reading, and reading widely. And the sort of reading and writing for change that I'm talking about here does not privilege nonfiction over fiction. Study after study demonstrates that the "deep" reading of fiction feeds the imagination, helps us to think, and builds empathy (Johnson et al. 2013, Belluck 2013, Murphy 2013). Nor am I referring to simple personal expression, with students simply pouring out their hearts on the page as though they are possessed by Tom Riddle's diary, followed by passive, unquestioning validation of this documentation of every mood. We don't have to stop there. We can ask writers to question. Why is this the way it is? How did it come to be this way? Who has power in this story? What does this power structure mean for the community? What makes you angry? What do you care about so very, very, much? Who is your community? Who do you feel alienated from? What does a "better world" mean to you? Katherine and Randy Bomer found that writers are naturally empowered when they are working as citizens "plugged into the world outside their classroom" (Bomer and Bomer 2001). They remind us that in teaching "personal" writing, educators have an opportunity to help student writers see the social and political themes in their work.

The mechanics and craft of writing can certainly be taught in this context; rigor absolutely complements the writing of clear, passionate, authentic work. But it is not always comfortable. In one of my favorite passages of literature, Queen Orual of C.S. Lewis' *Till We Have Faces* cries out, "Lightly men talk of saying what they mean. Often when he was teaching me to write in Greek the Fox would say, 'Child, to say the very thing you really mean, the whole of it, nothing more or less or other than what you really mean; that's the whole art and joy of words.' A glib saying. When the time comes to you at which you will be forced at last to utter the speech which has lain at the center of your soul for years, which you have, all that time, idiot-like, been saying over and over, you'll not talk about joy of words." Indeed. Good writing is work, meaningful, thoughtful, rigorous, risky work.

I've known a lot of teachers. I have never known one who did not strive daily to nurture this type of rich classroom experience. As I watch public school class size in New York City increase to more than thirty students in primary classrooms, teachers are demonized and disenfranchised by political gamesmanship; elected officials and administrators croak out feeble sound bites about standards, accountability, and yes, rigor. Nervous parents are told the myriad and costly ways in which our "failing" schools and teachers will be evaluated and assessed (Zimmer and Hamilton 2013), how our children will be efficiently transmogrified into numbers (Stern 2013), and that the commodification of public education is for the greater good. Meanwhile, time, resources, and attention to real teaching and learning seeps out like the air from a sad balloon at the end of a party (Neufeld 2013, Doostdar 2013). If we want our school communities to promote thoughtful, engaged citizenship, then all of us involved should be regarded as both teachers and learners, given room to operate in spaces of great possibility. Classrooms that promote writing as a tool for empowerment can facilitate creative expression and critical thinking. Classroom writers of all ages can examine themselves, their communities, the relationships among them, and how they negotiate those relationships.

None of this is a guarantee, of course, that we will automatically develop cadres of high-performing young writers and thinkers who will be the change they want to see and write all of us into a more perfect world. But, as the Bomers point out, we can be pretty confident that when we build communities that write to challenge, to hope, to imagine, to collaborate "in the midst of difficulty and diversity," we are engaged right now in the work of building a more just, more beautiful world.

So, goodbye for now, for the writing of this has given me ideas. I've got things to ponder, to worry over. I want to figure out what to do next. I'm a Black woman, a mother, a writer, a learner, and a teacher — and I'm allowed to wonder, to think, to dream, and do what I can.

So I'll write some more.

References

Baldwin, James. 1985. "A Talk to Teachers." Reprinted in *The Price of the Ticket, Collected Non-Fiction 1948–1985*. New York, NY: St. Martin's Press. (Originally delivered on October 16, 1963, as "The Negro Child—His Self-Image" and subsequently published in *The Saturday Review*, December 21, 1963.)

Belluck, Pam. 2013. "For Better Social Skills, Scientists Recommend a Little Chekhov." http://well.blogs.nytimes.com/2013/10/03/i-know-how-youre-feeling-i-read-chekhov.

Bomer, Randy, and Katherine Bomer. 2001. *For A Better World: Reading and Writing for Social Action*. Portsmouth, NH: Heinemann.

Bruer, John. T. 1993. *Schools for Thought: A Science of Learning in the Classroom*. Cambridge, MA: Massachusetts Institute of Technology.

Christensen, Linda. 2000. *Reading, Writing, and Rising Up: Teaching About Social Justice and the Power of the Written Word*. Milwaukee, WI: Rethinking Schools.

Davis, Joshua. 2013. "How a Radical New Teaching Method Could Unleash a Generation of Geniuses." *Wired*. October 16, 2013. www.wired.com/business/2013/10/free-thinkers.

Doostdar, Hassan. 2013. "Save Our Schools: Kids and Communities Fight School Closures in Chicago." *Indy Kids*, September 13, 2013. http://indykids.net/main/2013/09/save-our-schools-kids-and-communities-fight-school-closures-in-chicago.

Johnson, Dan R., Grace K. Cushman, Lauren A. Borden, and Madison S. McCune. 2013. "Potentiating empathic growth: Generating imagery while reading fiction increases empathy and prosocial behavior." *Psychology of Aesthetics, Creativity, and the Arts* 7 (3): 306–312.

Jones, Stephanie M., Joshua L. Brown, and J. Lawrence Aber. 2011. "Two-Year Impacts of a Universal School-Based Social-Emotional and Literacy Intervention: An Experiment in Translational Developmental Research." *Child Development* 82 (2): 533–554.

Murphy Paul, Annie. 2013. "Reading Literature Makes Us Smarter and Nicer." *TIME*. http://ideas.time.com/2013/06/03/why-we-should-read-literature.

Neufeld, Sara. 2013. "Set Up For Failure? New Standards, Exams Highlight School Resource Needs." *The Hechinger Report/Philadelphia Public School Notebook*. http://thenotebook.org/blog/136550/are-pennsylvania-students-being-set-failure.

Singer, Dorothy G., Roberta M. Golinkoff, and Kathy Hirsh-Pasek, eds. 2006. *Play = Learning: How Play Motivates and Enhances Children's Cognitive and Social-Emotional Growth*. New York, NY: Oxford University Press.

Stern, Gary. 2013. "N.Y.'s Teacher Evaluations Faulted in Study." *The Journal News*. October 15, 2013. http://www.lohud.com/article/20131015/NEWS/310150042/N-Y-s -teacher-evaluations-faulted-study.

Vega, Vanessa. 2012. "Social and Emotional Learning Research Review." *Edutopia*. www .edutopia.org/sel-research-learning-outcomes.

Wang, Shirley. 2009. "The Power of Magical Thinking." *Wall Street Journal*, December 22, 2009. http://online.wsj.com/article/SB10001424052748703344704574610002061841322 .html.

Zimmer, Amy, and Colby Hamilton. 2013. "First Day of School Means Start of Controversial New Teacher Eval System." *DNAinfo*, September 9, 2013. www.dnainfo.com/new-york /20130909/park-slope/first-day-of-school-means-start-of-controversial-new-teacher-eval -system.

Olugbemisola Rhuday-Perkovich *is often asked about her name; she is the daughter of a Nigerian father and a Jamaican mother, and married to a man of Croatian descent. She's the author of* Eighth-Grade Superzero *(2010), a contributor to* Open Mic: Riffs on Life Between Cultures in Ten Voices *(2013) and* Break These Rules: 35 YA Authors on Speaking Up, Standing Out, and Being Yourself *(2013), along with other works. She has also worked as a literacy educator, youth group leader, educational consultant, publicist, freelance writer, and is a member of PEN, SCBWI, and on the Advisory Board of Epic Change. Olugbemisola lives with her family in New York, where she loves to walk, cook, bake, knit, sew, and make a mess with just about any craft form. Please visit her website at: www.olugbemisolabooks.com.*

The UPLIFT Curriculum

Imagine a New Curriculum That Works for All

Marc Prensky

Almost all of today's education reformers' efforts to make education better focus on the HOW of delivering the current education. They ask, "How can the instruction of what we currently teach be improved?" and "Are there better ways to teach what we currently do?" The creators of the Common Core, for example, fall squarely into that camp: new standards for our old curriculum. And, to a certain extent, that is important.

But the far more fundamental change needed to truly make schools better is *not* just to how we teach. It is, rather, to *what* we teach. The world today is in desperate need of a wholly new curriculum. Why? Because our context has changed and our goals for education are changing. And with the curriculum we now have we can neither adapt to the new context nor reach our goals.

Currently, the entire world's curriculum is, at the highest level, fundamentally the same: it is some form of math, language, science, and social studies (or whatever those are called in different places). Because we have not offered any real alternatives, many have come to accept those four subjects — math, language arts, science, and social studies — as what "education" is truly about. That is why a program such as PISA can claim to compare and rank "the education" in countries across the world.

However, the assumption that education is only — or even mainly — about math, language arts, science, and social studies, and that there are no alternatives to this, is a false one. Moreover, this assumption has led the world, and the education of our youth, in harmful directions. We can — and I believe we must — do much better.

From Where Do They Come?

Today's four "pillars" of education — math, language arts, science, and social studies — are not ordained on high or by nature. Certainly those subjects go back a long way. In the United States at least, they were not codified as a "cannon" until 1892, when the so-called "Committee of 10" — ten college presidents, assembled by the National Education Association — recommended that they should comprise the bulk of the high school curriculum. The UK codified something similar, as the National Curriculum in 1988, and, by influence and copying, those became, in great measure, today's world curriculum. Additional subjects, such as art, music, physical education, hygiene, home economics, shop, and more recently, information technology — each with strong proponents — have at various times been added.

But almost all would agree that currently the four "main" subjects of math, language arts, science, and social studies (history, geography, sociology) are the key ones, that is, the ones we don't eliminate or relegate to after-school programs when money gets short.

And these days, the list is getting even shorter. Math, language, and science are often taking precedence in many places over the social sciences. That is what we offer, and generally require, for all our kids: math, language, and science. These subjects are what we seem to care most about. They are what PISA measures and compares. That is how we train, hire, and deploy all our teachers. The whole world is trying to "race to the top" of the "PISA pyramid" in math, language arts, and science. Science, technology, engineering, and math (STEM) are what's "in," despite a vocal subgroup pushing to make it STEAM (i.e., the above with arts included).

An Alternative

Having those four pillars — math, language arts, science, and some version of social studies — as the fundamental, top-level components, however, is NOT the only way to organize education. There are many other ways. And I think that, despite our history, some of those ways are far better, both for people in general and for the students of today and tomorrow.

I am not the first to think this. Many of our best schools — mostly independent ones — have been, for some time, emphasizing another side of education. Some call it "fundamental skills-based" or "character-based" education. Some define it as what people "are" — as opposed to what they know or even what they can do. I call it "becoming."

Those who support this type of education are, I believe, on the right track. Unfortunately, however, almost all of them do this *in addition to* teaching math, language arts, science, and social studies, not *instead* of teaching them.

I propose something very different.

The UPLIFT Curriculum

Suppose that instead of organizing our education at the top level by the four subjects of math, language arts, science, and social studies, and measuring and evaluating our kids who are only or mainly there (e.g., "How good are you in math?" "What's your verbal SAT score?" "Where is your country in science in PISA?"), we chose a different framework for our education.

Suppose we were to organize education — comprehensively from K–12 — around four very different top-level "pillars," or subjects. Suppose we were to organize education around the key things that are *actually important* to the success of every person in the world?

I believe that if we did this, those four subjects would be the following:

Effective Thinking
Effective Action
Effective Relationships
Effective Accomplishment

Those are the things that all people need to be good at in order to have a useful and successful life — no matter their location, work, or interests. Some may ask, "What do you mean by *effective*?" That adjective is not there to define it (it takes a huge variety of different forms) but mostly to distinguish it from *ineffective*. Most of us have learned to recognize those distinctions, although it's sometimes difficult and students need as much practice as we can give them in doing so.

So, with the qualifier of *effective*, Thinking, Acting, Relating, and Accomplishing are the four main subjects of the UPLIFT Curriculum. All students would study them as their four main subjects for thirteen years. They are what students would get assessed on and graded in. And, unlike the subjects of today, the names of those top-level subjects — Thinking, Acting, Relating, and Accomplishing — will make it very clear to students what their education is about, what they should become better at, and on what they will be evaluated.

What About Today's Subjects?

Math, language arts, science, and social studies will never go away. No one argues that they are important. Students will still learn these subjects, just not in the way they do today. The problem is that math, language arts, science, and social studies are not important *in the same way for everybody* — they are important in different ways, and to differing degrees, to each individual. But Effective Thinking, Effective Action, Effective Relationships, and Effective Accomplishment are important to all, and it is crucial that every student strive to get as good as they possibly can at each of them.

What's more, all of us know this. Parents know it, educators know it, and, most importantly, kids know it.

Of course every student is better at some subjects than at others, and every student will have a somewhat different profile of their UPLIFT Curriculum strengths. But knowing whether you are a person who is best at thinking or at acting, at building and maintaining relationships, or at accomplishing things in the real world is much more meaningful than knowing you are better at math, language arts, science, or social studies — certainly to a student and to their potential employers as well. Understanding people's relative strengths in thinking, acting, relating, and accomplishing is really how we all, in our heads, evaluate people. Grades in our current subjects, as well as personal recommendations and portfolio evaluations, are just proxies and evidence for what people really want to know.

Is There Enough There?

Perhaps you agree that Effective Thinking, Effective Action, Effective Relationships, and Effective Accomplishment are truly what's important. And further, you agree that they would be good candidates to replace math, language arts, science, and social studies at the top level of the curriculum — with the old subjects offered differently to different students.

Several questions might come to mind.

First, is there enough there? That is, is there enough in each of these four areas to keep students usefully engaged in learning about them for up to thirteen years? Second, what would the components of each main subject be? And third, how would we teach this curriculum?

Let me look at each of these in turn.

Effective Thinking

These are some of the components that would be in the Effective Thinking portion of the curriculum:

- Mathematical Thinking
- Scientific Thinking
- Critical Thinking
- Problem Solving
- Creative Thinking
- Design Thinking
- Systems Thinking
- Judgment
- Aesthetics
- Habits of Mind
- Self-knowledge of One's Own Passions and Strengths.

I believe almost anyone would agree that all of these are important. Today, other than the top two (or perhaps four at most) they are not in our K–12 curriculum.

Not that some teachers and some schools don't include some of these. But the only components we currently teach truly *systematically* — when we do — are mathematical thinking and scientific thinking (and more recently to a lesser, but hopefully growing extent, critical thinking and problem solving as well).

But all of the others, i.e., the extremely important thinking skills of Design Thinking, Systems Thinking, Judgment, Aesthetics, Habits of Mind, and Self-knowledge of One's Own Passions and Strengths (and, of course, the others too), are NOT taught systematically as part of the curriculum. Even the areas that are included are often taught more in terms of "content" than of "thinking."

One result is that we hear college teachers complain, over and over, "I have to teach my students to *think*." But college is not the time to do it — that is probably too late for many. Our students should be spending a large portion of their K–12 years learning, systematically, to think.

About What?

But, you might ask, to think about what? The answer is that it almost doesn't matter, as long as they learn to do their thinking well. There are some things, of course, that we would like all of our kids to think about — ethics and forms of government, for example — but most of the fundamentals of good thinking can be learned by considering situations and problems in whatever areas of interest each individual student has.

For example, I recently heard of a course that began with the question "Do people like me?" — a question that is likely to be of interest to all students. What that course was about was how to apply mathematical thinking to that problem. But students could learn, and practice, applying all the other forms of thinking to that question as well. *Any* problem of appropriate scope and level can be used to teach effective thinking. We would never run out of these.

The positive result of doing this is that we would focus our students' attention, in each domain, far less on the subject matter and far more on the way they approach thinking about it. Students would come out of this subject, after thirteen years, able to think about *almost any* problem or issue in multiple ways, wearing, as Edward DeBono puts it, multiple "hats" or "thinking caps." Young people would also be able to recognize that types of thinking were *ineffective*, something that today's kids are not, for the most part, great at.

The Big Missing Pieces in Our Current Curriculum

We can, and must, certainly teach the crucial subject area of Effective Thinking more specifically, more systematically, and better. But a huge part of our educational problem today is that most curricula are ONLY about thinking. Other huge domains, which are crucial for life and success — i.e., acting effectively, relating effectively, and accomplishing effectively — are almost entirely missing.

But not in the UPLIFT Curriculum.

Effective Action

Everyone is familiar with people who know lots of things but who can't do much. One reason for this is that we don't — or hardly ever — teach effective action in school. But we certainly could.

Thanks to Stephen Covey, for example, the *Seven Habits of Highly Effective People* have been known and recognized for more than a quarter of a century. What justification is there for our being aware of these incredibly important habits and yet not teaching them, systematically, to our kids? I use these habits every day and try to regularly practice them. (The Seven Habits are, in Covey's words: begin with the end in mind; do first things first; be proactive; seek first to understand, then to be understood; think win-win; synergize; and sharpen the saw.) I know them not because I learned them in school, but because I chose to remember them on my own after reading Covey's book. Today kids could learn and practice these habits in class — but they generally don't. Ironically, we even have good ideas about *how* to teach these habits, because the Covey Institute has developed a curriculum, which is used in some schools and places of work. But not in most places.

This is also true of the other components of Effective Action that we could and should be teaching our kids. These include: Positive Mindset, Resilience,

Entrepreneurship, Innovation, Project Management, Breaking Down Barriers, Improvisation, and more. Experts and curricula exist, but they are not part of our curriculum.

We often have our kids read *The Little Engine That Could* in kindergarten, but then we don't teach and build on the incredible power of a positive mindset for all their thirteen years. We may tell our kids we want them to be resilient, but we don't *teach* them resilience — a skill largely acquired over time, over our entire curriculum. There exists, in the world, curricula for teaching entrepreneurship and creativity, but few of our K–12 schools use them. Few K–12 schools, if any, include project management, a well-established discipline, anywhere in what they teach.

Again, we could do this. Doing so would be incredibly helpful. Imagine what our kids could accomplish if we did.

Effective Relationships

Relationships often come up in books, in projects, in classrooms, and in the course of our current curriculum. Yet how much of our curriculum is devoted to systematically analyzing those relationships, with the goal of making students better at building and maintaining their own effective relationships? Certainly little, if any. Yet the study of relationships is deep and well known, and many consider building and maintaining Effective Relationships to be the most important skill a person can possess.

Of course, we do help our kids with one-on-one relationships as they occur in the classroom (although not, generally, as part of the curriculum). But we could also be helping them become far more effective at building and maintaining relationships in teams, families, communities, workplaces, and, of course, online. We could also systematically help our kids be more effective at areas that depend on and help build effective relationships, such as Empathy, Ethics, Politics, Citizenship, Conflict Resolution, and Negotiation. For all of these there already exist curricula, created by various groups.

What if we made building and maintaining effective relationship a key pillar of the world's curriculum?

Effective Accomplishment

Of all the things missing from today's curriculum, our not teaching kids, systematically, about accomplishment in the real world is perhaps our greatest failing. That is because if we did, it could improve so much. Today, we essentially waste all the enormous potential "accomplishing power" of our youth, by not requiring them to use it.

Imagine, for example, if first grade in the world's poor villages was about building a cistern, if there wasn't one, and second grade was about building a water purification system. And third graders learned how to build a Wi-Fi system, and so on. This, of course, could apply to any place — just substitute whatever they need and are missing.

In former times, we stopped our kids from working in the real world because they were being physically exploited. But things are different now. All kids, even young kids, love to work on real, important projects. Most kids can figure out how to manage themselves, as individuals and in groups, particularly as they get older. Much of the work to be done in the world today no longer requires physical work, but rather intellectual work (e.g., on computers). Students of all ages, joined together by our increasingly powerful networks, could be accomplishing enormous numbers of desperately needed things — not just in their local areas, but in nations, businesses, and even across the world. All of these projects would be giving them powerful and valuable educational experiences.

The Role of Technology

UPLIFT is a curriculum for the future. Yet you may have noticed that up until now I have not written a word about technology.

Why is that?

The answer was given to me several years ago by a high school student, when he told me: "You guys [adults] think of technology as a tool. We think of it as a foundation — it underlies everything we do."

Technology's role is to be a foundation and support for everything we do. The entire UPLIFT Curriculum is supported by and bathed in technology — technology which, these days, is rapidly and continually improving.

The four elements of the UPLIFT Curriculum — Effective Thinking, Effective Action, Effective Relationships, and Effective Accomplishment — always remain the same. But every day, technology allows students to do new things in each of those four domains, as well as to do old things faster and better.

We would make a mistake, though, if we allowed kids or the curriculum to focus first and foremost on technology. The focus should always be kept, rather, on Effective Thinking, Effective Action, Effective Relationships, and Effective Accomplishment.

The Role of Teachers

Who should be doing this? Teachers, of course! Even with technology, teachers still play a huge and important part in the UPLIFT Curriculum. We desperately need good teachers, and they will always have an important role to play. But teachers' jobs and roles will never again be the same as they were in the past or are now.

Because so much can now be done with technology, and because this ability will continue to improve rapidly, we no longer need our teachers to be the distributors of content — certainly not content about math, language arts, science, and social studies. Technology can already do a satisfactory job, and soon will do a great job, of distributing all of our content in more and more good, participative, and creative ways, to students who need it. Today's Khan Academy and Massive Online Open Course (MOOCs) are some of our first examples of this, but they should be viewed as, and evaluated as, only our very first baby steps.

What we need teachers for, rather, are the many things that technology *can't* do well or can't do at all. Those things include motivating our students, respecting them, empathizing with them, and encouraging their individual passions.

Motivation, respect, empathy, and passion cannot — at least for the foreseeable future — come from machines. Those are the *human* traits needed for a successful education, and they are the things we require our human teachers to provide.

As we — hopefully — reorganize our curriculum around Effective Thinking, Effective Action, Effective Relationships, and Effective Accomplishment, we will need to train our teachers differently. Teachers will no longer train to be specialists in math, language arts, science, and social studies, but rather as specialists in each of the four new top-level areas. Reflect, for a moment, about which of these four new domains — thinking, acting, relating, and accomplishing — YOU might like to specialize in and/or teach. Why?

Why "UPLIFT"?

Why do I call this new curriculum that is based on Effective Thinking, Effective Action, Effective Relationships, and Effective Accomplishment the UPLIFT Curriculum?

An important role of any new curriculum we establish will be to stop the endless chase for higher grades and for better ways to teach the old subjects of math, language, science, and social studies to all. There is, in fact, no need to do this. Those subjects are just proxies for the real supporting skills that lie under them.

Countries and schools around the world have been teaching the old curriculum for years, with almost nothing to show for it — at best, small gains or minor adjustments in PISA rankings. The world's education is, in general, getting not better, but rather worse — all because, I believe, we are teaching the wrong things.

My hope is that there will be some countries in the world — as there are already some individual schools — that will be interested in getting off this futile treadmill and moving to something better.

If they do — and if they offer their students a curriculum based on all students being the best they can be at Effective Thinking, Effective Action, Effective Relationships, and Effective Accomplishment — my belief is that their students will leapfrog others and quickly become better than those places that don't. That is, those students, and places, will be "uplifted."

Which will be the first country to do this? My guess is that it will not be the nations at the top of the PISA list. But when we begin to do it, and when, as a result, we have better measures of where kids are succeeding at the things that really count, such a world will look very different.

The Goal of Education

Underlying our need to change the curriculum is a new, or revised, understanding, not just of our changed context, but also of what education is *for* in our society — of what its goal actually is.

If asked about the goal of education, many educators (and other adults) would tell you it is "learning." Almost all of the books in the Education section are about some type or method of learning. "Learning" is what we try to measure in our assessments. And we often refer to our students as "learners."

But learning is NOT the real goal of education. Learning is only a MEANS to the real goal of education, which is "BECOMING" — becoming a good, competent, and flexible person, who will help make the world a better place.

"Becoming" is, or should be, the goal of education in the world. Unfortunately, until everyone realizes this and acts on it, much of the huge amounts of time and money the world now spends on education will remain, essentially, wasted.

It is my great hope that by moving to something like the UPLIFT Curriculum, and by focusing our young people on, therefore, the *true* basics, i.e., Effective Thinking, Effective Action, Effective Relationships, and Effective Accomplishment (rather than on what we teach kids today), the world will take giant steps toward the goal of effectively educating all its people, and, therefore, toward making the world a better place for all of us, and our posterity, to live.

Marc Prensky, *author of the 2001 article "Digital Natives, Digital Immigrants," is an internationally acclaimed thought leader, speaker, writer, consultant, and game designer in the field of education and learning. He is the author of five books:* From Digital Natives to Digital Wisdom *(2012),* Teaching Digital Natives: Partnering for Real Learning *(2010),* Don't Bother Me, Mom, I'm Learning *(2006),* Digital Game-Based Learning *(2001), and* Brain Gain: Technology and the Quest for Digital Wisdom *(2012). Marc is the*

founder and CEO of Games2train, a game-based learning company whose clients include IBM, Bank of America, Pfizer, the US Department of Defense, and the L.A. and Florida Virtual Schools. He is also the co-founder of Spree Learning Games, a new "curricular games" company. Marc holds an MBA from Harvard and a masters in teaching from Yale. Many of his writings can be found at: www.marcprensky.com /writing. Contact Marc at marcprensky@gmail.com.

PART **3**

Imagine Better
Support for Teachers

With a Compassionate Gaze

Thoughts on Acceptance, Artistry, and the Teaching We Hold Dear

Deb Kelt

Remembering my years teaching middle and high school, memories float back: Juan reading a picture book about garden gnomes, his blue/black tattoos complicated and beautiful opposite the elves' red hats; Karina and Tatiana arguing passionately — in English and Spanish — about *Keesha's House*, a flurry of thinking, laughter, and occasional shouting; Montell's silly walks and uncanny imitations that dissolved any lesson into fits of laughter; Alejandro's tears after he didn't pass our state's writing test ("I just want to be a writer," he said, and then we told him he already was); the way Maribel's face lit up as she talked about her daughter — her "*pequeño sol*"; the cards my students sent after a beloved family member died unexpectedly, urging me to keep my head up, that things would get better.

These moments were filled with a togetherness I struggle to define. In each memory, our shared humanity seemed undeniable, a thread of compassion that stitched us together no matter the circumstances — the lighthearted and difficult, the complicated and simple. An unconditional acceptance underscored our best days, a sense that we were in this together. We could celebrate our happy times. We could weather our struggles. We could figure things out.

I didn't build this environment on my own. My mother — my first teacher — provided the greatest lessons in unconditional love. Her hand was in many of these moments, because I first learned compassion from her parenting. The writings of Randy and Katherine Bomer have deeply influenced my teaching as well. The power of appreciative lenses — affirming what kids do well, finding their "gems" (K. Bomer 2010), celebrating and developing every student's varied and beautiful abilities — is the centerpiece of my teaching.

And my students — how to describe the many things they taught me? Their friendship, their laughter, and their honesty helped build our classroom. As they pushed on through difficulties — Hurricane Katrina, family members left behind in Mexico, the personal anxieties of adolescence — they helped me see struggle in a different way. Their strength taught me about perseverance, a lesson I in turn redirected toward their academic work. When the reading and writing were difficult, we found ways to negotiate these struggles. We weren't "bad" at these skills, we were encountering normal rough patches. We talked through the tangled bits. We created charts to remember our strategies. And we practiced keeping our heads up, even when the work got hard.

But there was a dropped stitch in the cloth we were creating. Though my lessons attempted to banish the labels my students had heard for years — that they were "struggling," that they were "behind" or somehow "deficient" — I applied those very labels to myself and my instruction. While I steered my students toward a notion of learning that insisted knowledge is not static but is ever changing and growing, never "done," I expected my own teaching to be perfected and finished, my practices encased in amber. I showed my students the messiness of drafting and revision, yet I recoiled when my own lessons didn't play out perfectly. Looking back, I see I excepted my professional efforts from every educational commitment I held dear. I did not see the good in my teaching. Self-analysis and reflection revealed only deficits. I spent too many car rides home counting the things that had gone wrong that day. I did not accept my struggles and hardships as normal, denied myself hope that things could get better, and lacked compassion about my own teaching. The irony still baffles me: I pushed forward an appreciative stance toward my students and their academic work while pulling it away from myself and my own professional endeavors.

Broadening Our Appreciative Lenses

The deficit lenses through which we view ourselves are just as damaging as the deficit lenses through which we view our students. If students flourish under an appreciative gaze, it follows that we can also grow professionally under that same gaze: "Doctor, heal thyself." Recently I read an article by Dr. Kristin Neff (2011) about the power of self-compassion — treating ourselves with kindness, being "gentle and understanding with ourselves rather than harshly critical and judgmental." To be self-compassionate, Neff states, human beings must recognize our "*common humanity* . . . rather than feeling isolated and alienated by our suffering." We must be mindful of our experiences. We must "hold our experience in balanced awareness, rather than ignoring our pain or exaggerating it."

All of these ideas spoke to me as a teacher. I had berated myself about my work, sometimes daily. I rarely shared the difficulties I experienced, which made me feel isolated and alone. I exaggerated my shortcomings, worrying that things would completely fall apart. A mini-lesson gone awry could make me question the efficacy of an entire unit, sometimes an entire semester. Instead of seeing my struggles as self-contained, even normal aspects of teaching, my deficit tendencies often triggered a spiral of shame in which fear and self-doubt flourished — I obsessed about the test, worried about my students and their progress, fretted about who might not walk across the stage at graduation if my work fell short. Panic made it hard to think clearly and solve problems. I often shut down.

Self-compassion is not merely an excuse for one's imperfections — it has concrete benefits. With an attitude of self-compassion, human beings can weather difficult times. Neff states, "When our sense of self-worth stems from being a human being intrinsically worthy of respect — rather than being contingent on reaching certain goals — [it] is much less easily shaken." Mistakes don't become catastrophes, praise seems less important, and a sense of shame never enters the picture. Instead, self-compassionate people "take things in stride," thinking "'everybody goofs up now and then'" (Neff 2011). I argue that self-compassion is critical to battling teacher fatigue, burnout, and the onslaught of negativity that teachers often face in a system where test scores reign supreme. Furthermore, self-compassion can help us see the true nature of our work. Sometimes — oftentimes — teaching is just plain hard.

But even as I write these words, the practice of self-compassion feels difficult and far away. Ending a bad day with an "oh-well" shrug makes my stomach churn, perhaps because the stakes are so high and we have so many students under our care and instruction. (When I taught high school, I sometimes had 150 students.) We have big goals — we want each student to soar — and every moment is precious. Many of the students in my classrooms would be the first in their families to graduate from high school. Some had literally walked to the United States from Mexico. Their dreams were epic, and it seemed irresponsible to not be harsh about my teaching efforts.

Nevertheless, I take a breath and wonder if perhaps it's the other way around. If we are serious about seeing what "every student does brilliantly and beautifully," if we want to name "what is and how perfectly that works for now," if we trust that where each child is in this moment is undeniably "enough" (in her beautiful book *Hidden Gems*, Katherine Bomer calls this "a blessing"), we must also "bless" ourselves. If we want to teach these things, we must practice these things — as with so much in our field. We write so we can teach writing. We read so we can teach reading. We must see the good in our work so we can see the good in our students' work, otherwise our efforts are diluted. If we are serious about every child reaching his or her goals — and if we stand by our belief that these goals can be reached when we start from strength — there can be no exceptions. Not even for ourselves. We must be models of self-love and compassion rather than martyrs constantly self-flagellating and repenting.

Self-compassion will help us persevere and grow as teachers. When we embark on new teaching challenges — a genre never tackled before, a conferencing strategy just discovered in a professional book — we can let go of perfectionist tendencies and accept our missteps with grace, just as we do with our students. When others dismiss our work, we can share the complex processes of our pedagogy. When we are frustrated with colleagues, we can turn our appreciative lenses toward them, too, and find the good. If we accept one another while also embracing our struggles, we can work together more effectively and solve problems.

This will require courage, because speaking about teacher frustrations feels a little like blasphemy, like breaking some sort of teacher code. As Richard Hawley (1979) wrote, ". . . the experience of teaching imperfectly is essentially a private matter. And . . . because failure is by nature humiliating, we tend to keep it to ourselves." But if we accept struggle as a normal part of our profession, not as a signifier of our worth as a teacher or a human being, perhaps we can be more comfortable strategizing and sharing. We can find ways to make our work better and stronger. Energy spent on shame can instead be directed toward inquiry, a way to see our work as unfinished, evolving, growing. No more hiding behind pristine lesson plans and perfected final drafts — no more denying that struggle exists — but rather we can focus on becoming a community of seekers that speaks honestly and deeply about the work we hold dear.

Reclaiming Teaching as a Creative Act

Self-compassion becomes easier when we frame teaching as a creative act. I have lived with an artist for twenty years, and in all that time I have rarely heard him berate a piece in process. Instead, the work is "coming along," in need of "more color," or simply "unfinished." He often says the same about his friends' or his brother's work. There is always more to do. When my husband is working on a piece, he positions it across the room and gazes at it from the couch for long moments. This can go on for days. "There is a lot of paper crumpled up in wastebaskets for writers, there are lots of canvases that are painted over for painters, and lots of lousy experiments that get run by scientists," says psychologist Dr. Art Markman (2013) of creative endeavors. Acceptance of the process — the time it takes to make something beautiful — is a huge part of creative work.

Teaching is indeed a creative act. Every August we envision and plan our school year, just as a painter may roughly sketch out a landscape she has imagined. We have certain directives to follow (district and national standards), and yet we find ways to make these prescriptions sing in our classrooms while we discover ways to maneuver within or around them (as so many artists break with tradition to discover something beautiful and new: Jackson Pollock, Frida Kahlo, Claude Monet, to name just a few). We worry about connecting with our audience, because like artists, actors, and musicians, we know our work matters only when it is shared. If we are English teachers, we practice the art of writing; we study the work of other writers. Both our content and our pedagogy are steeped in creativity. Sometimes it's hard to tell where one stops and the other begins, like an Escher drawing, a hand drawing a hand that is drawing another hand.

At a recent NCTE convention, I heard a new teacher lamenting the condition of his first-year planbook. He couldn't believe how many cross-outs it contained, how many arrows pointed elsewhere, how many erasures. But that's like an artist's sketchbook — like the pages I saw years ago at a museum in Paris, sketch after re-sketch after resketch as Picasso planned his masterpiece Guernica. My brother-in-law, John, told me this about a recent painting: "I had this piece, and there were seven or eight colors on it. I thought, this isn't working. It's got too much color. So I simplified it." The mistakes were important. The mistakes helped him get it right. "I had to do that."

That's the mental picture I want to carry of myself as a teacher — a teacher who is an artist, a "creative intellectual" (Zapata 2013), a teacher who experiments and grows and sketches again and again, progressively more pleased with what I uncover but always still working, still growing, not "finished yet" (R. Bomer 2011). I want to hold up my work like my husband does — study it, inquire into it, redo it, revise it, rethink it. I want to be invested in these difficult patches — the times when my teaching feels betwixt and between — not be destroyed by them. I want to have open conversations with colleagues and administrators, so together we can reimagine these struggles and create something powerful and new. I want to accept that there are more questions than answers and that it may take years for me to find some of these answers — a lifetime, perhaps.

I want to reconsider my mini-lessons as tiny etchings, with tight lines and intricate details, designed to move learning ahead in a meaningful, profound way. I want to consider my school a community of creators, a collective of both teachers and students. I want my conferences to be improvised jazz solos — like the riffs of John Coltrane or Ella Fitzgerald — in which I think on my feet, research quickly, connect with and teach each student, while the rest of the class keeps humming. I want to look at my year's work as a grand composition, a chapter in a book I am still writing, still revising, still holding dear.

As the artist Sister Corita Kent (1992) said, "Nothing is a mistake. There's no win and no fail. There's only make."

I want to let go of winning and failing. I want to be a teacher who makes.

References

Bomer, Katherine. 2010. *Hidden Gems*. Portsmouth, NH: Heinemann.

Bomer, Randy. 2011. *Building Adolescent Literacy in Today's English Classrooms*. Portsmouth, NH: Heinemann.

Hawley, Richard A. "Teaching as Failing." *The Phi Delta Kappan* 60 (8): 597–600.

Kent, Corita, and Jan Steward. 1992. *Learning by Heart*. New York, NY: Bantam Books.

Markman, Art. "Why Creative Minds Think Alike." *Two Guys on Your Head*, KUT/NPR, aired December 13, 2013. http://kut.org/post/why-creative-minds-think-alike.

Neff, Kristin. 2011. "Why Self-Compassion Trumps Self-Esteem." *Greater Good*. May 27, 2011. Retrieved December 10, 2013. http://greatergood.berkeley.edu/article/item/try_selfcompassion.

Zapata, Maria A. "Examining the Multilingual and Multimodal Resources of Young Latino Picturebook Makers." Dissertation, August 2013, University of Texas, Austin, TX.

Deb Kelt *taught middle and high school reading for more than twenty years. She is now a lecturer at the University of Texas at Austin, currently teaching adolescent literacy in the department of Curriculum and Instruction. Deb is also the co-director of the Heart of Texas Writing Project at the University of Texas at Austin.*

The Gratitude That Support Built

Samantha Bennett

Teaching and learning take a tremendous amount of energy.

As an instructional coach, my job is to support teachers as an energy catalyst—setting up the structures to spark, expand, and sustain that energy over time.

How do I know if this catalysis has an impact? One of the markers is the presence of gratitude.

Why gratitude? According to positive psychologists, the expression of gratitude is key to a happier, more meaningful life. In 1998, Martin Seligman, as head of the American Psychological Association, started a scientific and professional movement in order to " . . . explore what makes life worth living and building the enabling conditions—happiness, flow, meaning, love, gratitude, accomplishment, growth, better relationships—[that] constitute human flourishing." Most would agree that "human flourishing" is also a vital purpose of K–12 education—and a great reason to get out of bed in the morning.

Catalysis. Energy. Flourishing. Gratitude. What does this look like in schools? What structures best support teachers so they can't help but express gratitude? Read on to find out.

The Players (in order of appearance):

DAWN: Eighth-grade social studies teacher

LINDSAY: Dawn's teammate, also an eighth-grade social studies teacher

SAM: Instructional coach

JANE: Eighth-grade student

JENNY: Principal

KARI: District Executive Director

(With all due respect to the British nursery rhyme "This Is the House That Jack Built")

---

1 I love this sentence from Dawn's email because it speaks to four of the most important beliefs I hold as an instructional coach:

> This is the gratitude Dawn felt.

- Belief #1: Teachers need to do the bulk of the intellectual work — coaches can't do it for them.
- Belief #2: Coaches have a role as an authentic audience for teacher work.
- Belief #3: Reflection is a key component of teacher (and student) growth and effectiveness.
- Belief #4: Empathy is at the root of effective coaching.

From: Dawn
Date: May 17 11:06 AM
To: Sam
Subject: Re: What a day!!!

Thanks for believing in us and challenging us to be better. I truly feel like I was reborn as a teacher this year, and I know Lindsay and I give you a TON of credit for that. I know we did the work, but you nudged us, supported us, cheered us on, believed in our kids, and celebrated with us, and that makes all the difference.[1] **1** We are looking forward to working with you this summer, and any future chances we get to see you and ask you questions, and beg you for help! We absolutely are in love with you and can't express how appreciative we are for all you have done to help us this year. We were so lucky to get this experience and we will never forget it.

Thanks, hon!
Dawn :-)

Reflection takes time, but it is time well spent because it gives teachers energy, and it ensures that students don't get the "first draft" of teachers' planning, assessment, and instruction. The questions "Where are we going?" "Where are we now?" and "How can we close the gap?" (Stiggins et al. 2011) are at the heart of the research on closing the achievement gap for students. They also live at the core of teachers' most important work — planning for student learning.

There are several structures I can put in place as a coach to help a teacher reflect in answer to these questions. The most direct way is to ask them to write to me AFTER I put in the time to write to them. After every visit to a classroom, I immediately email the teacher a coaching note that labels the student learning I noticed, a few things I wondered about, and ends with the phrase, *"What are you thinking? Just type for five minutes and press send."* If they don't write back I have to consider, "Was the email boring? Did I give them anything interesting to think about or a reason to write back to me?"

Once the practice of writing to reflect becomes a habit, there is no stopping the cycle of continual improvement — because teachers reflect for the benefit of their students — not for me. They also tend to build more time into their lessons for students to reflect — which, research says, is another key to maximizing student learning (Stiggins 2011).

Over time, teachers continue to write to me because I respond, in conversations and in writing. I show them I am paying careful attention to their thinking and using it as a basis for future instruction. Again, it's a practice they begin to parallel with their students — using daily formative assessments to inform instruction along the way.

As a coach, prioritizing my role as an "audience for reflection" meets a teacher's basic human need for connection — it builds a relationship of trust and empathy — and it helps teachers act smarter for their students every day. Teachers send me check-ins years after our work together has ended. All humans crave an authentic audience.

2 Another belief shines through these lines:
- Belief #5: We are better together.

Focusing on the students — on their talk, their thinking, and their work — is the greatest leverage point for coaching conversations (Sweeney 2013). When feedback revolves around the students, it keeps everyone focused on what matters most. Teachers and coaches become partners and coconspirators to do whatever it takes to help students succeed; "we are better together" becomes the mantra.

3 Planning backward, with the end in mind and a connection to the real world, is central to this type of work (Wiggins and

> This is the praise Sam showered on
>
> That prompted the gratitude Dawn felt.

On Thu, May 16 at 11:16 PM, Samantha Bennett <sambennett2@yahoo.com> wrote:

Hi Lindsay and Dawn,
Wow! What a day! It is late, and I hope you are all snuggled up in your beds and dreaming about the amazingness of your students today — seeing them deliver their civil rights speeches up on their soapboxes — loud and proud and knowledgeable and passionate, and wanting do-overs, even! I talked to so many students who said, "I'm going to do my speech again and speak louder and clearer so more people hear what I have to say!"**[2]** They will remember this for the rest of their lives. I just know it. I will, for sure.

I am in awe of the two of you and your dedication and perseverance to pull this off — 240 civil rights speeches in the middle of downtown Denver?!**[3]** I was bragging about you in Ohio yesterday, and the teachers made me promise to send some of the photos. You are an inspiration to teachers all over the country!**[4]** I can't wait to read ALL of the students' civil rights speeches next week.**[5]**

xo,
Sam

McTighe 2005). A sense of the impossible makes it compelling and irresistible — and the connection to the real world makes this a BIG goal, impossible to reach alone: "What do civil rights activists do? How do they spend their time? What do they read? What do they create to have an impact on the world? How can I help all 240 students do this? Hmm . . . I'm going to need some help. This is too big to do all by myself." If our goals are too small, we don't need each other. We are better together.

4 We are connected to the world in lots of ways: the Internet, Twitter, blogs, etc. We can't plan in a vacuum, detached from the world. We should never plan in isolation. There are resources, ideas, inspiration, and texts — lots and lots of texts — everywhere. We are better together.

5 Focus on the students' work to gauge if learning has occurred and what's next. This is another way a coach can be an authentic audience — by being another set of eyes to look at students' work. We are better together.

6 Belief #6: Learners need high-quality models — a vision of what they are aiming for — in order to ensure and maximize growth.

We used high-quality models all the way through this project, starting with a model for the vision of the final performance-based assessment — Speakers' Corner in Hyde Park, London. Students watched videos of different speakers in Hyde Park to gauge their tone, pacing, and attempts to engage their audience. They also analyzed famous civil rights speeches throughout American history, to look at word choice, flow, content, and the connection between claims and support. Students' speeches had to meet these learning targets:

- I can describe how political rights connect to social and economic rights in the United States.
- I can state a focused argument for a civil rights issue.
- I can use well-chosen details to support my claim.
- I can use the vocabulary of historians and civil rights activists in my talk and in my writing.
- I can synthesize historical (and other) texts in order to support my argument about current civil rights issues.
- I can speak out in public to educate an audience about a civil rights issue.
- I can use engaging eye contact, volume, and clear pronunciation to engage my audience.

All those goals for learning were great, but they all hinged upon the question, "Where would we get enough soapboxes for students to stand on?" Ha! It took a few phone calls, but we finally found a grocery store willing to lend us some milk crates. Whew. Crisis averted.

This is the soapbox stood upon[6]
That led to the praise Sam showered on
That prompted the gratitude Dawn felt.

6

The teachers needed models too, examples of high-quality learning targets and matched assessments built into a unit of learning, framed around big ideas. After analyzing other similar units, the teachers spent an entire day planning this quarter-long unit to be sure it met the eighth grade social studies standards while also incorporating history, civics, and economic content standards.

Lindsay (Dawn's teaching partner) also functioned as a model for her colleagues. Lindsay graciously opened her classroom door to her colleagues so we could use her classroom as a "text" to help us get smarter. We framed a day of learning together, with Lindsay's instruction as the main event. We started with a pre-brief, where Lindsay shared her teaching beliefs, the goals of the unit, and where the day's lesson sat within her big goals. Next, we observed her students at work and took careful notes on what we saw and heard and why it mattered to student engagement. After the lesson, we debriefed and labeled what we saw with connections to research on motivation, engagement, and learning. In the afternoon, the focus shifted back to our own classrooms, where we planned lessons incorporating the practices that each teacher believed matter most to the students' growth. This model will be familiar to some as Lab Classroom Professional Development, a format pioneered by the Denver-based Public Education and Business Coalition (PEBC). What we know from research and experience is that this type of job-embedded professional development helps teachers grow. Everyone needs a model (Sweeney 2011, 2013; Stiggins 2011; Black and Wiliam 1998).

7 Belief #7: High-quality work takes multiple drafts. Students deserve more than our first-draft thinking.

Jane wrote this speech over several weeks. As she crafted her argument, she needed to read to build her background knowledge and find support for her argument, as well as get feedback from her peers and her teachers to know if her argument was compelling and clear. Over these weeks, Lindsay and Dawn taught a series of focused mini-lessons dedicated to helping Jane meet each of the learning targets. One of the keys to making sure that ALL students are able to meet learning targets is "lessons focused on one aspect of quality at a time" (Stiggins 2011).

One of the ways to ensure students have enough time — time to build background knowledge, tackle new genres and levels of complex text, write in new genres with increasing sophistication, and revise to make sure their message is clear and compelling to a reader — is to plan longer units. This gives students time to wrestle with the text, to make meaning for themselves, and to create meaning for others.

We are never "done" with planning for student learning. It is essential that teachers take time to plan both long-term units and also day-to-day as students are immersed in the content. While students study content, we study them — how are they making meaning and what do they need next to grow? It is an iterative process, and we should build in chunks of time to do multiple drafts of our planning process in order to have the greatest impact on our students' learning.

We lose 50 percent of teachers in their first five years in the profession (Lambert 2006). In my experience, this is due to the

This is the speech about civil rights [7]
Voiced by a student with all her might
On high from the soapbox stood upon
That led to the praise Sam showered on
That prompted the gratitude Dawn felt.

Thank you for stopping by and listening to my speech. There is an issue that I think is very important and probably affects most of us here today. Gender equality. The law states that men and women should get paid equally for equal work. But that doesn't happen. Men in Colorado earned an average $50,997 compared to women who earned an average of $40,236, an earnings ratio of 79 percent. Because of this it could be making my life more difficult. My mom works six days a week, full-time. My dad is currently a student at CU Denver and works once or twice a week for a few hours. In this situation my mom brings in most of the money, and sometimes it gets hard to provide for all of our family's needs. Imagine this: A single woman with two small children. She works full-time, five days a week, and has trouble taking care of her kids because she doesn't get paid as much as a man would that has the same job and hours as her. What can you do to help people like her or me and maybe even yourself? Make a change.

Some women do act and try to make a change by going to court. The Equal Pay Act was declared by John F. Kennedy in 1963 to be the end of the "unconscionable" practice of paying female employees less wages than male employees for the same job. . . .

hamster-wheel pace of the work. They teach a full day, giving every ounce of energy they have. After the students leave, teachers go to meetings, coach teams, grab a quick bite to eat, and then ask themselves the dreaded question, "What am I going to do tomorrow?" We need to help teachers plan in longer chunks — at least three weeks at a time — so they may prioritize goals, focus on what students will make to demonstrate their understanding, and design a context for the content that matters most. Then, on a daily basis, instead of asking the question, "What am I going to do tomorrow?" teachers could ask, "What will the students do tomorrow to move them closer to the long-term goal I set for their learning?" Students deserve more thoughtful, revised-over-time planning for their learning. Students deserve more than our first-draft thinking.

Imagine a school where all teachers have time to plan like Dawn and Lindsay had — eight long, focused, connected hours (every quarter!) — time to envision and plan the framework of this type of unit, from beginning to end. Imagine if they had time to gather high-quality models; a variety of compelling, complex texts for their students to read; and time to thoroughly think through and devise persuasive reasons for students to read those texts, such as a variety of interesting guiding questions that would help the students interrogate the content instead of just consume it. Imagine what might be possible for our students if we took that kind of time to plan. Just imagine.

8 | Belief #8: Whoever is doing the reading, writing, and talking, is doing the learning.

This foundational belief is a high-leverage entry point for increasing substantive learning in every classroom. We talk about a lesson within a pie-chart structure because the goal is that for two-thirds of the class period students are reading, writing, talking, problem solving, etc., to "get smarter." The shaded part of the pie represents students' work time. When teachers plan to maximize the number of minutes that students are not only behaviorally engaged (doing what we ask them to do, when we ask them to do it) but they're also emotionally and cognitively engaged, learning happens (Bennett 2007).

One way to know if students are cognitively engaged is to ask them to make their thinking visible every day, either through talk or through writing. This means students need to make things each day (formative assessments) and teachers need to look at what students make each day to see what they understand *and* what they need next to grow. This is the basis for differentiation, individualized learning, and maximizing growth for each learner. If students "make" worksheets with the same answer in every slot, it doesn't really give teachers the kind of feedback they need to plan for future instruction. As John Hattie writes in *Visible Learning* (2009) " . . . feedback was among the most powerful influences on achievement. . . . The mistake I was making was seeing feedback as something *teachers provided to students* — they typically did not. . . . It was only when I discovered that feedback was most powerful

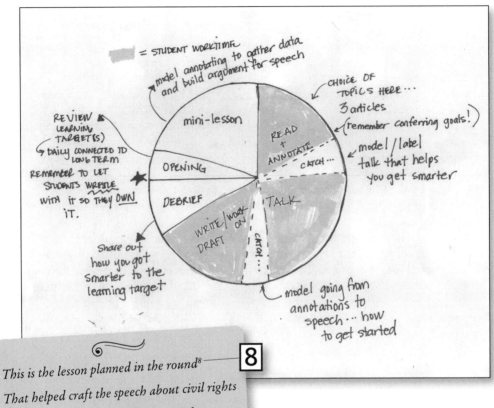

This is the lesson planned in the round[8]
That helped craft the speech about civil rights
Voiced by a student with all her might
On high from the soapbox she stood upon
That led to the praise Sam showered on
That prompted the gratitude Dawn felt.

when it *was from the student to the teacher* that I started to understand it better" (12). In order to get great "feedback" from students about what they are learning, teachers have to thoughtfully *plan* to get layered, nuanced responses from students about what they are figuring out each day. Both what they understand and what they are questioning and confused about. That is the only way to know what students might need to read, write, and talk about *next* to build their knowledge, skills, and understanding.

Belief #9: Teachers must look at students' work on a daily basis in order to maximize each student's growth over time.

Feedback from students about what they understand and how they are making meaning is essential to future lesson design. One of the most straightforward ways to see what students "get" is to ask them to annotate text (Tovani 2011).

Annotations help students consciously use thinking strategies when meaning breaks down, helps them talk back to the text, and prioritize their own thinking — alongside the author's thinking. It helps students hold that thinking over time, so they can use it to create new works — like civil rights speeches with a claim, support, and a call to action!

Annotations help teachers understand how students are determining importance, what vocabulary they need to become more sophisticated readers and writers, and what future text they need to sink their teeth into to get even smarter. It helps teachers get to know how each student's brain functions, what they care about, and where they get stuck and shut down. Teachers can't ensure individual student growth and learning without this type of feedback from students.

Women And Equal Pay: Wage Gap Still Intact, Study Shows

The Huffington Post | By Christina Huffington Posted: 04/09/2013 9:55 am EDT | Updated: 04/09/2013 2:18 pm EDT

[handwritten: 50 YEARS & STILL NO EQUAL PAY]

On April 9, 2013, we celebrate the 50th anniversary of the Equal Pay Act of 1963, which President John F. Kennedy declared to be the end of the "unconscionable practice of paying female employees less wages than male employees for the same job" when he signed it.

[handwritten: DOESN'T seem like it]

The anniversary, known as Equal Pay Day, marks how far into 2013 women must work to earn what men earned in 2012. That doesn't exactly sound like the Equal Pay Act achieved its goal, does it?

[handwritten: WOW-UNFAIR]

Women in the United States today are paid on average 77 cents for every dollar paid to men -- *[handwritten: Now are they racist?]* the gap is even worse for African-American and Latina women -- and according to a new study done by the National Partnership For Women And Families, the gender-based wage gap exists in every state and in the country's 50 largest metropolitan areas.

The NPWF study analyzed U.S. Census Bureau data -- the first ever analysis by metropolitan area -- and found that the wage gap -- the median yearly pay for women who are employed full time is $11,084 less than men's -- has major implications for their ability to afford essentials like food, housing and gas. *[handwritten: WOW-Because that effects my life. Mom works full time dad only works 2 days of the week.]*

If the gap was eliminated in Seattle, the metropolitan area with the worst wage discrepancy, the study showed, women would be able to afford 2.3 year's more worth of food. In New York City, women could afford seven more months rent (for those of you who live in New York, you know how *huge* that is). In Austin, a woman could afford 2,369 additional gallons of gas. *[handwritten: full time college student.]* *[handwritten: eliminate it every where!]*

The list goes on and on and on -- go check out your own city or state on the NPWF website -- but the point is that the money being withheld from women is not a trivial matter. The situation is

---

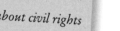

This is draft one where the student expounds[9]
Influenced by the lesson planned in the round
That helped craft the speech about civil rights
Voiced by a student with all her might
On high from the soapbox she stood upon
That led to the praise Sam showered on
That prompted the gratitude Dawn felt.

9

To: Lindsay, Dawn
From: Sam
RE: Lindsay & Dawn Planning 4.22

Hi Lindsay and Dawn,
It was great to listen in on your planning today. You are developing habits that are having HUGE payoffs for your students.[10]

10

Your thinking about, "Are we going after rights or issues?" is the exact same conversation we want students to have. Your intellectual and emotional rigor is an incredible model for your hopes of students' intellectual and emotional rigor.

I'm going to label some patterns of planning I saw you practice today:

- Wrestling with the wording of the learning target to ensure students walk away with a deep understanding of the content. Today you settled on: I can identify political rights and the social and economic effects of those rights. Bravo!
- Planning backward for the daily lesson: starting with the TARGET — then to the WORK TIME, then back to the mini-lesson, forward to the debrief. Bravo!
- Finding a compelling text for students to read and working through your own process of making meaning of the text to meet the target — thinking out loud to make sure the annotating you model is what you want students to replicate and expand upon during the work time. Bravo!

Other structures we discussed today to help propel this unit powerfully toward the civil rights soapbox speeches on the 16th:

- Share the actual, physical calendar with kids. Show them the number of days they have until they are going to be speaking about their civil rights issue on the streets of downtown Denver.
- Post students' names (and photos if you can!) next to the topics they want to do a soapbox speech about.

- Start collecting articles (and have students start to look for articles) that will help them get smarter about their topic. Have folders full of accessible articles that kids can pull from in order to start to get "fed" about their topic. This will be great for differentiation and engagement.
- Think about layering a writing day (or two) into the next two weeks of school desegregation content to make the soapbox speech ever-present in their minds and give them a reason to dig into the school desegregation texts . . .

Have fun today. I can't wait to see the annotations and exit tickets the students create. I'll see you Wednesday.

Talk soon,
Sam

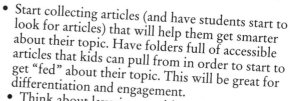

This is feedback that prompted the plan
To get to a draft where the student expounds
Influenced by the lesson planned in the round
That helped craft the speech about civil rights
Voiced by a student with all her might
On high from the soapbox she stood upon
That led to the praise that Sam showered on
That prompted the gratitude Dawn felt.

10 | Belief #10: All learners crave feedback because working toward mastery is at the heart of human motivation (Pink 2009).

If teachers don't respond to feedback, we need to look in the mirror instead of blaming them. As Susan Brookhart (2008, p. 30) writes, "You know your feedback is effective if:
- Your [teachers] do learn — their work does improve.
- Your [teachers] become more motivated — they believe they can learn, they want to learn, and they take more control over their own learning.
- Your [school] becomes a place where feedback, including constructive criticism, is valued and viewed as productive."

11 | Belief #11: The focus of leadership matters to teachers' growth.

What do the leaders of a school care most about? How do you know? Jenny Edgerley, the principal of Northglenn Middle School, cares most about student engagement. She spends every minute of every day SHOWING that care by noticing, highlighting, and supporting student and teacher learning, student and teacher growth, and student and teacher risk taking. Immediately after Lindsay and Dawn created their plan for the Civil Rights Unit and shared their vision with Jenny, she put the date for the speeches on her calendar and didn't let any other meeting, appointment, or crisis interfere with her ability to make it downtown to hear the students' speeches.

Before they went downtown, Jenny spent time in the classrooms to be an audience for the students to practice and to give them critical feedback. Each time she was in the classrooms, she left Dawn and Lindsay notes sharing what she'd heard from students and what she noticed about their growth. She let Dawn and Lindsay know that she appreciated their focus on student engagement, that they were bringing their curriculum to life for students, and that they were taking a huge risk by bringing 240 students to downtown Denver. She let them know she had their backs and that they were changing students' lives each day they took a new risk in their planning, assessment, and instruction to meet students' needs and promote students' growth — as learners and as human beings.

Jenny's work "behind the scenes" also backs up this vision. The school schedule is organized around big chunks of time for students and teachers to do the work that matters most. She dedicates a huge part of her budget to professional development and prioritizes time for teachers to plan together, look at student work together, and reflect on student learning together. She takes risks as a learner herself, like planning a science unit "backwards" and implementing that unit by being a guest teacher in a classroom for two weeks so she better understands what she is asking her teachers to do. She understands and honors the complexity of teaching and learning and doesn't pretend there are quick fixes for the challenges teachers and students face on a daily basis. She is a model for the kind of person we all want to work with, work for, and be. Visionary leadership matters to teachers' growth.

This is the principal being a big fan [11]
Of supportive feedback that helps teachers plan
To get to a draft where the student expounds
Influenced by the lesson planned in the round
That helped craft the speech about civil rights
Voiced by a student with all her might
On high from the soapbox she stood upon
That led to the praise that Sam showered on
That prompted the gratitude Dawn felt.

12 | Belief #12: Gratitude matters.

Hi Jenny,

Please feel free to extend this to your amazing eighth-grade team and students! Thank you for allowing me to come and watch your incredible students take risks by presenting their soapbox speeches downtown yesterday. They were, simply, inspiring!

The planning, reflection, energy, enthusiasm, and dedication demonstrated by your teachers is to be commended. I read through the planning template, and it got ME excited about teaching and the possibilities! This was after listening to them and hearing their unbridled enthusiasm about what they had created for and with their students when we sat in their sharing session last week. Very impressive!

This is District thanks for lives being changed
By teachers and their principal, who's a big fan
Of supportive feedback that helps them plan
To get to a draft where the student expounds
Influenced by the lesson planned in the round
That helped craft the speech about civil rights
Voiced by a student with all her might
On high from the soapbox she stood upon
That led to the praise that Sam showered on
That prompted the gratitude Dawn felt.

I wanted to share a quick story with you regarding my conversation with a couple of the students. I talked with quite a few . . . they were so proud, even the young lady who forgot her speech. We talked about the fact that she took the risk to get up on the box — we didn't see any adults doing that — and what she learned and was passionate about when writing her speech. I think she walked away with a different perspective rather than, "I just failed."

Jeremy was not only amazing in the delivery and message of his speech, but the reflection as to what brought him to that place. I asked him how long he and his classmates took to prepare for the presentations. He let me know it was about a couple of weeks. Then I asked him how his teachers prepared him and his classmates. Take a deep breath and grab a couple of tissues. . . .

"Well, Miss. They believed in us. That is what gave us confidence to share our voice."

Thank you, NGMS, phenomenal teachers, and administration. You are doing more than teaching. You are inspiring learning and touching hearts and lives beyond just today. Thank you. It is an honor to be working alongside you.[12] — 12

With deep respect,
Kari
Executive Director of Schools
Adams 12 Five Star School District

> *This is the cycle of support that shouldn't be strange*
> *To get to the thanks for the lives being changed*
> *By teachers and their principal, who's a big fan*
> *Of supportive feedback that helps them plan*
> *To get to a draft where the student expounds*
> *Influenced by the lesson planned in the round*
> *That helped craft the speech about civil rights*
> *Voiced by a student with all her might*
> *On high from the soapbox she stood upon*
> *That led to the praise that Sam showered on*
> *That prompted the gratitude Dawn felt.*

Structures That Promote School-wide Gratitude

- An authentic audience for reflection

- Learning abs and other classroom-based, job-embedded professional development structures

- Looking at student work to drive goal-setting and planning

- Big chunks of time for long-term planning (e.g., an entire eight-hour sub day, per quarter)

- Observations and feedback based on student learning goals and student talk and work

- Focus on the number of minutes students are "doing the work" each classroom period. Work to maximize the number of minutes and students' behavioral, emotional, and cognitive engagement during those minutes. It is only in the intersection of the three types of engagement that learning is maximized (Fredericks et al. 2004).

- Rituals and routines that tap into the keys to human motivation (Pink 2009):

  ◊ **autonomy** — by increasing teachers' choice, voice, and ownership of their daily work through curriculum design — building relevant context around standards to help make content come alive for learners (Dobbertin 2013)

  ◊ **mastery** — developed by allowing time for careful lesson design, study, and feedback and chunks of time for the intellectual work of planning and looking at student work — not just at "scores" — to consider the implications for the next day, the next week, and the next month

  ◊ **purpose** — linked to a cause larger than ourselves. Visionary administrators like Jenny and Kari who help teachers focus on what matters MOST: the continual formation, reformation, and inspiration of the next generation of problem solvers, social activists, readers, writers, thinkers, designers, scientists, mathematicians, citizens, and "better humans" who will help realize and further the goals of our democratic society.

Beliefs That Ground These Practices

- Belief #1: Teachers need to do the bulk of the intellectual work — coaches can't do it for them.

- Belief #2: Coaches have a role as an authentic audience for teacher work.

- Belief #3: Reflection is a key component of teacher (and student) growth and effectiveness.

- Belief #4: Empathy is at the root of effective coaching.

- Belief #5: We are better together.

- Belief #6: Learners need high-quality models — a vision of what they are aiming for — in order to ensure and maximize growth.

- Belief #7: High-quality work takes multiple drafts. Students deserve more than our first-draft thinking.

- Belief #8: Whoever is doing the reading, writing, and talking, is doing the learning.

- Belief #9: Teachers must look at students' work on a daily basis in order to maximize each student's growth over time.

- Belief #10: All learners crave feedback because working toward mastery is at the heart of human motivation (Pink 2009).

- Belief #11: The focus of leadership matters to teachers' growth.

- Belief #12: Gratitude matters.

References

Bennett, Samantha. 2007. *That Workshop Book: New Systems and Structures for Classrooms That Read, Write, and Think.* Portsmouth, NH: Heinemann.

Black, Paul, and Dylan Wiliam. 1998. "Inside the Black Box: Raising Standards Through Classroom Assessment." *Phi Delta Kappan* 139–148.

Brookhart, Susan. 2008. *How to Give Effective Feedback to Your Students.* Alexandria, VA: Association for Supervision and Curriculum Development.

Dobbertin, Cheryl. 2013. *Common Core, Unit by Unit: 5 Critical Moves for Implementing the Reading Standards Across the Curriculum.* Portsmouth, NH: Heinemann.

Duhigg, Charles. 2012. *The Power of Habit: Why We Do What We Do in Life and Business.* New York, NY: Random House.

Fredericks, Jennifer A., Phyllis C. Blumenfeld, and Alison H. Paris. 2004. "School Engagement: Potential of the Concept, State of the Evidence." *Review of Educational Research* 74 (1): 59–109.

Hattie, John. 2009. *Visible Learning: A Synthesis of Over 800 Meta-Analysis Relating to Achievement.* New York, NY: Routledge.

Lambert, Lisa. 2006. "Half of Teachers Quit in First Five Years." *Washington Post.* www.washingtonpost.com/wp-dyn/content/article/2006/05/08/AR2006050801344.html.

Pink, Daniel. 2009. *Drive: The Surprising Truth About What Motivates Us.* New York, NY: Riverhead Books.

Seligman, Martin. 2011. *Flourish: A Visionary New Understanding of Happiness and Well-being.* New York, NY: Simon & Schuster.

Stiggins, Rick, Jan Chappuis, Steve Chappuis, and Judith Arter. 2011. *Classroom Assessment for Student Learning: Doing It Right—Using It Well,* Second edition. New Jersey: Pearson, Inc.

Sweeney, Diane. 2013. *Student-Centered Coaching at the Secondary Level.* Thousand Oaks, CA: Corwin.

———. 2011. *Student-Centered Coaching: A Guide for K–8 Coaches and Principals.* Thousand Oaks, CA: Corwin.

Tovani, Cris. 2011. *So What Do They Really Know?: Assessment That Informs Teaching and Learning.* Portland, ME: Stenhouse.

Wiggins, Grant, and Jay McTighe. 2005. *Understanding by Design,* expanded 2nd ed. New Jersey: Pearson.

Samantha Bennett *is an instructional coach, writer, and educational consultant based in Denver, Colorado. She is thankful to the administrators, teachers, and students of Northglenn Middle School for the opportunity to be inspired by their brilliance, vision, and days filled with hope, laughter, and endless possibility.*

Learning to Teach in the Twenty-First Century

Linda Darling-Hammond

For as long as she could remember, Elena had always wanted to teach. As a little girl, she would sit and read to toddlers, round up her friends to play "school," and explain the mysteries of the universe to anyone who would listen. She loved the feeling she got as a peer tutor in middle school when her partner learned something new in math or science. She loved finding games for her fellow students to practice with and resources for their projects on the school's CD-ROM databases. She loved finding fascinating books online and then, in a rush of excitement, running to the library to retrieve them.

Elena's community service project in high school allowed her to work as a teacher's aide in an elementary school classroom. There she began to look with real interest at the variety of ways young children seemed to learn and the many different interests they brought with them to school. She linked up with other high school students engaged in similar projects through an Internet group started by Future Teachers of America. She had the feeling she could spend a lifetime studying children and their unique paths to learning without ever running out of new mysteries and insights.

When she finally arrived at college, Elena knew she would want to prepare to teach, so early in her sophomore year she began taking courses in developmental and cognitive psychology. To qualify for an eventual teaching license, she also needed to select a major in an academic discipline. Elena chose mathematics because she had always enjoyed the structures and patterns of mathematical ideas and problems. By her junior year, Elena had decided to pursue the five-year course of study that led to a master of arts in teaching at her university. After a round of interviews and a review of her record thus far, Elena was admitted into the teacher education program. She was slated for an intensive program featuring coursework that was tightly linked to practice, including an internship in the professional development school sponsored by the university and the local school system.

In her courses, Elena immersed herself in the educational philosophies of thinkers like Emile Rousseau, John Dewey, and Maria Montessori while she also inquired into how children grow, learn, and develop. She had never before considered that there might be differences in views about the purpose of education, and she began to wonder what her own views were and would become. She studied developmental theories from Piaget to Vygotsky while she was conducting a semester-long case study of John, the seven-year-old boy she tutored in a local neighborhood school. As Elena watched John at play and at school, sometimes in person and other times on videotape, she could see the developmental theories coming to life before her eyes. Her case study raised questions that inspired her to read further and engage in long discussions with her professor and fellow seminar students. They talked about how John's physical and social development intersected with his academic performance, and how all of these could be supported and stretched. She was puzzled by his facility in some areas, like the use of geometric ideas and the construction of models, and his struggles with others, like extended reading. She carried these puzzles with her into her other courses as she worked to understand learning.

In these courses, Elena had the opportunity to examine other case studies of children who learned in ways similar to and different from the ways she had documented in her case study of John. Many of these cases were available on a hypermedia system that allowed her to see videotapes of individual children and classrooms over time, to call up samples of children's work, records about their learning, and documentation from their teachers about their learning strategies, problems, and progress.

Elena could search these databases for information about different learners, and she and her classmates could evaluate and discuss them in order to develop a grounded sense of how students progress, what different learning approaches look like, and how children develop various intelligences: verbal, logical-mathematical, visual-spatial, musical, kinesthetic, interpersonal, and so on (Gardner 1985). It was in one of these sessions that Elena had her first insight into her case-study student, John, understanding how he might be more adept at visual-spatial, geometric tasks and less comfortable with verbal ones. She began to think about what a teacher could do to use John's strengths to create productive pathways into other areas of learning.

In her mathematics courses, Elena was engaged in learning and applying mathematical ideas and studying how people learn mathematics. She undertook projects that engaged her in mathematical modeling and computer simulations; statistical analyses; and interdisciplinary projects with students in engineering, architecture, and the social sciences. These allowed her to deepen her understanding of mathematics and to examine the range of applications that would be important to her future student mathematicians, as well as to her.

In addition, these courses were linked to the work she was doing in cognitive psychology. Elena kept a journal of how she herself learned mathematics — what kinds of teaching strategies made the concepts more accessible to her and what things mystified her — and she interviewed fellow students about their experiences, including "math-phobics" who found the field difficult or terrifying. In her other courses, including those in areas she found difficult, she also kept track of the kinds of learning experiences that helped her understanding and those she found hard to fathom. In her electronic journal, she created her own database about learning experiences — one that would later allow her to look back and investigate how she learned, what was important for her learning, what created problems for her, and how she responded to them, both academically and emotionally.

Over time, as she studied how people learn and develop physically, psychologically, socially, and academically, Elena began to understand how children are influenced by their environments and how they make sense of the world. Her courses included practical applications that required her to observe and work with students in elementary, middle, and high school settings, as well as in out-of-school situations like recreation centers and community sites. Because of these opportunities to apply her learning, Elena never found theory dull or abstract. To the contrary, she found it gave her a powerful set of lenses to bring to the world of teaching and learning.

Building on what she had already learned about human development, Elena found her courses in teaching strategies and curriculum development fascinating. In courses that modeled the kinds of strategies she herself would be using as a teacher, she looked at ways to engage students in experiences that would help them create challenging products, integrate skills into hands-on activities, and conduct their own inquiries and experiments. Professors rarely lectured from textbooks or measured learning by end-of-unit tests. Instead, they created learning opportunities that enabled students to apply their learning in the context of real teaching situations. These were frequently enacted in the professional development school (PDS) where Elena was engaged in a yearlong internship under the guidance of a team of university- and school-based teacher educators.

In the professional development school, Elena was placed with a team of student teachers led by a team of expert veteran teachers in a school that had committed itself to providing state-of-the-art preparation for prospective teachers as well as cutting-edge education for children. Elena's team of student teachers included one with a concentration in art, another in language arts, and a third in science, in addition to her teacher in mathematics. They were able to discuss learning within and across these domains in many of their assignments and to construct interdisciplinary curriculum together.

Most of the school- and university-based teacher educators who comprised the PDS faculty had been certified as accomplished practitioners by the National Board for Professional Teaching Standards, having completed a rigorous assessment that required them to complete performance assessments and assemble a portfolio of evidence about their own teaching. The team of school- and university-based faculty created courses, internship experiences, and an accompanying team-taught seminar that allowed them to integrate theory and practice, pose fundamental dilemmas of teaching, and address specific aspects of learning to teach.

Located in a port city that served a broad range of racial, ethnic, and economic groups, as well as recent immigrants from more than forty countries, the professional development school enabled new teachers to learn how to support learning for new English language learners and to examine teaching from many cultural perspectives. In her seminars linked to classroom work as an intern, Elena looked at ways to identify and address a variety of learning styles and needs, including visual, aural, and kinesthetic approaches to learning; ways to address misconceptions students might hold about specific subject-matter concepts; and approaches to common challenges, like dyslexia, that require special teaching strategies. She learned how to construct lessons and use teaching strategies that would allow pathways for different kinds of learners.

Under the guidance of a mentor team, Elena's classroom work included observing and documenting specific children; evaluating lessons that helped illustrate important concepts and strategies; tutoring and working with small groups; sitting in on family conferences; engaging in school and team planning meetings; visiting homes and community agencies to learn about their resources; planning field trips and curriculum segments; teaching lessons and short units; and ultimately largely taking responsibility for the class for a month at the end of the school year. This work was supplemented by readings and dialogues grounded in extensive cases of teaching. A team of PDS teachers videotaped all of their classes over the course of the year so that they could serve as the basis of group discussions of teaching decisions and outcomes. These teachers' lesson plans, student work, audiotaped planning journals, and reflections on their lessons and lesson outcomes were also available — mostly in a hypermedia database organized to link to each lesson. With real teaching cases to work with, the student teachers could look at practice from many angles; examine how situations in the classroom arose from things that had happened in the past; see how various strategies turned out; and understand some of the teacher's thinking about specific students, subjects, and curriculum goals as she made decisions. Because the PDS was also wired for video and computer communication with the school of education, master teachers could hold mini-seminars and conversations with the student teachers by teleconference or email when on-site visits were impossible.

In her classroom work, research, and case studies, Elena learned how to look at and listen to students so as to understand their experiences, prior knowledge, and learning strengths as well as their difficulties. She learned how to provide emotional support and teaching strategies that were responsive to their needs. She learned how to create engaging tasks that would stretch and motivate students, and how to scaffold the learning process so students could then succeed at this challenging work. She began to learn how to juggle and balance the competing demands of individuals and groups, curriculum goals and student interests, supports and challenges. She learned how to reach out to students who might otherwise slip past or fall through the cracks. She learned to question and learn from her own teaching and that of her colleagues.

In the professional development school, Elena learned how to design authentic learning opportunities for her future students and how to evaluate and support her own learning. Whereas her future students' products were the essays and books they would write, the debates and performances they would stage, the scientific experiments they would design and conduct, Elena's exhibitions were the curricula she designed, the research she conducted into classroom and school practices, the inquiries she launched about the community around the school, and the lessons she taught. She maintained a portfolio of her work — case studies of students, research projects on particular teaching questions, curriculum designs, videotapes of herself teaching, analyses of others' teaching, and samples of student work connected to discussions of her teaching over time. Some of this work, including videos of her teaching, was assembled in an electronic portfolio that would allow the state licensing agency and future employers to evaluate aspects of her work as a supplement to face-to-face interviews and licensing examinations.

When Elena finished her rich, exhausting internship year, she was ready to try her hand at what she knew would be an equally demanding first year of teaching. She submitted her portfolio for review by the state professional standards board and sat for the performance examination that would grant her an initial teaching license. She was both exhilarated and anxious when she received an offer to teach in a school near the PDS where she had prepared. While nervous, Elena was comforted by the fact that her cohort of fellow graduates, along with one of her former professors and a mentor teacher from the PDS, would all be available to her in a study group throughout the year. They planned to stay connected by monthly meetings and an online network where they could talk, post questions, and share ideas and materials.

Elena spent that summer eagerly developing curriculum ideas for her new class. She had the benefit of advice and insights from the district mentor teacher already assigned to work with her in her first year of teaching and an online database of teaching materials developed by teachers across the country and organized around the curriculum standards of the National Council of Teachers of Mathematics, of which she had become a member. Later in the year, she could access curriculum writers and users of these online materials to discuss why and how they had designed and used particular ideas in certain ways and to think through how they might be adapted to the needs of her students.

Elena's mentor teacher worked with her and with several other new middle school mathematics and science teachers throughout the year, meeting with them individually to examine their teaching and provide support. The mentors and their first-year colleagues also met in groups once a month at the professional development school to discuss specific problems of practice. These meetings kept Elena connected to many of her peers and teachers from the university as well as to a group of expert veteran teachers across the district who brought with them many different kinds of expertise. With these resources and those of her teaching team at the middle school, Elena never felt as though she was alone in her efforts to tackle the many challenges of beginning teaching. She always had colleagues to turn to for advice, counsel, and support.

Elena found that the most engrossing part of her initiation to teaching was the students. She was as delighted and intrigued by their interests, energy, and different approaches to thinking as she had been when she was a student herself. Although she found teaching challenging, she did not feel overwhelmed by classroom management and discipline issues the way beginning teachers once had. Her extensive internship and ongoing mentoring had really prepared her to establish a well-functioning classroom from the start, and she had experience developing engaging curriculum and using a range of teaching strategies to draw upon.

She met weekly with the other math and science teachers in the school to discuss curriculum plans and share demonstration lessons. This extended lunch meeting occurred while her students were in a Project Adventure/physical education course that taught them teamwork and cooperation skills. She also met with the four other members of her teaching team for three hours each week while their students were at community service placements, working in local businesses, public agencies, a senior citizens center, and the elementary school and day-care center that shared their school building. The team used this time to discuss teaching plans, interdisciplinary connections, and the progress of the eighty students they shared. In these two different settings, Elena had access to her colleagues' knowledge and thinking about both subject matter issues and student concerns. They learned together about curriculum, pedagogy, and student learning.

When a concern arose about a particular student's progress, teachers in the team would hold a descriptive review session in which to examine the student's work and behavior using their pooled experiences and insights to identify areas of strength, approaches to learning, family contexts, and needs. The student's advisor would contribute information from individual student and family conferences, while other teachers added their observations from interactions in and out of class. Elena found that these sessions not only helped her learn about particular students and ways to address their needs, but it also helped her understand learning in general, and it gave her ways of looking at and listening to students that strengthened her teaching.

In addition to these built-in opportunities for continual learning, Elena and her colleagues benefited from the ongoing study groups they had developed at their professional development school and the extensive PD offerings at the local university and Teachers Academy. The study groups, which met during the school's staff development sessions (typically on Friday afternoons while students were in their academic clubs), were created by the school's Staff Development Committee and were based on the faculty's interests. Different groups were created each year, each led by a faculty member, sometimes with the participation of interested faculty from other schools or from the university. Each group had funds to purchase books, curriculum materials, or consulting help. This year's groups were looking at strategies for supporting the inclusion of learning disabled students in mainstreamed classrooms;

improving the teaching of research skills for students' graduation portfolios; implementing the state's new mathematics and science curriculum standards; and understanding language development for new English language learners. Elena was attending the last of these because she had several children in her classes who were recent immigrants and she wanted to know more about how to help them learn mathematics.

At the Teachers Academy, school- and university-based faculty taught extended courses in areas ranging from advances in learning theory to all kinds of teaching methods: elementary science, interdisciplinary topics in the humanities, uses of mathematics in the teaching of social studies, writing across the curriculum, advanced calculus, and much more. These courses usually featured case studies and teaching demonstrations as well as follow-up work in teachers' own classrooms. Multimedia conferencing allowed teachers to "meet" with each other across their schools and to see each other's classroom work. They could also connect to additional courses and study groups at the university, including a popular master's degree program that helped teachers prepare their portfolios for National Board Certification. The Academy provided technologies needed for hypermedia learning platforms, for online conferencing, and for televised classroom observation. It also provided connections to many of the networks that teachers and principals used to create professional learning communities for themselves, such as the National Writing Project, the Urban Mathematics Collaborative, the Foxfire Teacher Outreach Network, and the Coalition of Essential Schools.

Elena knew that all of these opportunities would be available to her when she was ready for them. With the strength of a preparation that had helped her put theory and practice together, and with the support of so many colleagues, Elena felt confident that she could succeed at her life's goal: becoming — and as she now understood, always becoming — a teacher.

Reference

Gardner, Howard. 1983. *Frames of Mind: The Theory of Multiple Intelligences.* New York: Basic Books.

Linda Darling-Hammond *is Charles E. Ducommun Professor at Stanford University, where she founded and co-directs the Stanford Center for Opportunity Policy in Education. She was founding executive director of the National Commission on Teaching and America's Future and headed President Obama's Education Policy Transition Team. Her most recent book,* Getting Teacher Evaluation Right, *makes the case for a research-based approach to teacher evaluation and provides guidelines and models to make it happen.*

Key Principles of Learning to Become, by Luke Reynolds

In Linda Darling-Hammond's beautiful vision above, of Elena's fictional journey to become a teacher, we see keys to powerful, creative, rigorous, and imaginative teacher-preparation programs. Primarily, all of the steps — outlined below — that are explored in Elena's journey are steps of **becoming***. Embedded in every part of a teacher's journey is the constant reminder that teachers are always becoming — always journeying, never fully arriving. This notion is in direct contrast to the arguments of market-industrialism and of seeing schools as merely input-output systems. Instead, schools — both K–12 public education systems and teacher-preparation programs like the one Elena went through — are empowered by complex human relationships, connection, and authentic learning and growth. Elena's journey shows us the following key needs for imagining teacher-preparation programs in the twenty-first century:*

1. **Teacher preparation program are rigorous.** Those who enter such programs do so with great passion and enthusiasm, like Elena, but they must be challenged deeply with new learning, new ways of thinking, and new ways of seeing themselves, the world, and their students. These challenges are not always easy, and they require immense time and energy.

2. **Teacher preparation programs are intensely reflective.** As we have seen, Elena must complete a number of reflective practices during her program, and even after it, as a full-time teacher. Case study explorations of students, linking theory to practice, videotaped teaching experiences, and journaling are all components of this beautiful reflective practice.

3. **Teacher preparation programs are active.** Elena cannot learn about students and about her own abilities and needs as a teacher if she is insulated within a college classroom. Nor can she learn if her university professors do not model the dynamic, connected, and vibrant nature of learning and teach to various learning styles. Instead, Elena encounters a number of incredible opportunities to apply her learning and to experience life as a teacher, beginning in small doses, and then gradually increasing her responsibilities in accordance with her growth. The university and the school are in communication, and an ethos of active, engaged growth sustains this connection. The expectations for Elena are that she will be deeply involved with the students, the school, her college, and her mentors.

4. **Teacher preparation programs are essential.** Instead of going a short, quick route to teaching, Elena engages in informed, active, reflective, and empowering practices of learning to become a teacher. This preparation enables her to enter the classroom as a confident, committed, and capable new teacher. While she will still struggle — as all new teachers do — Elena will have the added benefit of a strong foundation and a huge network of support. And Elena will also possess the key knowledge that struggle is natural and normal — she has already experienced this often in her teacher preparation program. Elena will see her struggles and growth as a teacher as part of her *becoming*, rather than as markers of her failure. Elena will be inspired and committed to keep growing and learning, in her first year as a teacher or in her thirty-fourth.